LINES

Volume One

SIGHT READING
and
SIGHT SINGING EXERCISES

By
Bruce Arnold

Muse Eek Publishing Company
New York, New York

ISBN 1-890944-76-9

Printed in the United States

This publication can be purchased from your local bookstore or by contacting:
Muse Eek Publishing Company
P.O. Box 509
New York, NY 10276, USA
Phone: 212-473-7030
Fax: 212-473-4601
http://www.muse-eek.com
sales@muse-eek.com

Table Of Contents

Acknowledgments

The author would like to thank Michal Shapiro for proof reading and helpful suggestions. I would also like to thank my students who through their questions helped me to see their needs so that I might address them as best I could.

About the Author

Bruce Arnold is from Sioux Falls, South Dakota. His educational background started with 3 years of music study at the University of South Dakota; he then attended the Berklee College of Music where he received a Bachelor of Music degree in composition. During that time he also studied privately with Jerry Bergonzi and Charlie Banacos.

Mr. Arnold has taught at some of the most prestigious music schools in America, including the New England Conservatory of Music, Dartmouth College, Berklee College of Music, Princeton University and New York University. He is a performer, composer, jazz clinician and has an extensive private instruction practice.

Currently Mr. Arnold is performing with his own "The Bruce Arnold Trio," and "Eye Contact" with Harvie Swartz, as well as with two experimental bands, "Release the Hounds" a free improv group, and "Spooky Actions" which re-interprets the work of 20th Century classical masters.

His debut CD "Blue Eleven" (MMC 2036J) received great critical acclaim, and his most recent CD "A Few Dozen" was released in January 2000. The Los Angeles Times said of this release "Mr. Arnold deserves credit for his effort to expand the jazz palette."

For more information about Mr. Arnold check his website at http://www.arnoldjazz.com This website contains audio examples of Mr. Arnold's compositions and a workshop section with free downloadable music exercises.

Foreword

There is a direct correlation between a student's ability to identify pitches and their musicality. This ear training series presents a method with which I have had great success in improving my students' abilities to identify pitches, and provides a way to take one more step on the journey toward master musicianship.

Bruce Arnold

New York, New York

How to Use this Book
For Beginners

There are many methods of ear training available to the serious music student. I call the method used hear "relative pitch ear training," but it is not based on interval training or on memorizing melodies to be regurgitated back at the instructor. What makes this ear training different is that a student memorizes the sound of all 12 pitches against a key center. There are steps and exercises required to reach this first plateau. Each of the 12 pitches we use in western music has a distinctive sound when heard against an established key center. If we were to play a I IV V I progression in the key of "C" a few times over this would establish a key center in the listener's mind. If we then play one of the 12 available pitches this note would have a distinctive sound against that key. For instance, if we play an "F" note it sounds like the fourth. Now, this is not because it is a fourth interval above the tonic, it is because it has the unique sound of the fourth degree. We should'nt derive the answer by singing out loud or thinking up from the tonic in our mind. And lastly and most importantly we shouldn't think or sing "Here Comes the Bride" to get to that fourth interval. These common tricks are taught in many schools and while they may work to get a student through a test to pass a course, they don't train a student's ear to hear what pitches are going by when music is played in time.

So if we don't use these age old tricks, what to we do to develop good relative pitch? If you try the example above and find you have to use any of the aformentioned crutches then you have an ear training problem which needs to be addressed.

As I said earlier, we recognized the "F" pitch because we recognize the sound of the fourth of the key. There are two levels that you need to work on to get your ears working properly. One is singing, the other is listening. As far as the listening is concerned I highly recommended that you work with the "Ear Training: One Note" method books/CDs in combination with this book. Please see the back of this book for details and ISBN number for these books. You could also make yourself a tape (or have someone test you) that plays a I IV V I progression in C and then plays any note. You should listen to the note and guess what you think the note is. If you have no idea what the pitch is <u>guess</u> . DO NOT RESORT TO THOSE CRUTCHES for identifying the pitch. If you find you are guessing a lot don't worry; you will improve with time. The idea is to hear these pitches over and over again until you just recognize the sound. It is best if you practice this tape many times throughout a day for short 10 or 15 minute periods. This is because you need to keep these sounds in your short term memory as much as possible. Over time your permanent memory will take over remembering these sounds.

The other thing to practice is singing exercises. This will help you to start internalizing each of the 12 pitch against a key. Start with the single line melodies found in this book and sing them over a major chord which should be sounding at all times. This major chord should be based on the root of the key, i.e. in "C" major play a "C" chord. Use the solfeggio for each note: "do, re, mi, fa, sol, la, ti, do." If you flat a note it is an "ay" sound, so "mi" flatted would be sounded "may." The exception is "re"-- if you flat that note it is sounded "raw" If you sharp a note it is an "ee" sound so "fa" sharped is "fi"

When singing these exercises try to prehear each note; don't just let your voice slide around to the pitches but try and hear each note in your mind first. If you try to hear a note in your head and hear nothing don't worry-- you will start to hear these pitches over time and much practice. Never play a note before you at least try to sing it. This method will ultimately help to alleviate problems later.

As you progress you can start to work on the 2 through 4 part lines found in this volume. I wouldn't however start on these other exercises until you can play I IV V I in "C", play any note and recognize it quickly and accurately.

How to Use this Book
For Advanced Students

After you have reached the ability to hear any of the 12 pitches against a key it is time to move on to 2 notes against a key and to start singing the exercises found in this book that incorporate 2, 3 and 4 voices. It is recommended that you use the Ear Training: Two Note Method books to work on two note ear training. These books entitled Ear Training: Two Note can be found in the listing at the end of this book.

To master hearing more than one note at a time you need to work on it from two different standpoints. Once again you should use a taped exercise and the singing examples in this volume incorporating the 2, 3 and 4 note part singing. But first you need to understand some of the possibilities that happen when more than one pitch is heard simultaneously. When doing 2 note ear training with a tape (or someone playing two notes) you need to follow a specific number of steps to do it properly. Start by playing I IV V I in the key of "C"; then sing the tonic of the key (or hold this pitch in your head) which would be a "C" note. You then need to play two notes simultaneously while continuing to sing or think the "C" note. Don't concentrate on the 2 notes you hear but concentrate on the tonic pitch "C" that you are singing. Listen to see if you still hear this pitch as the tonic For instance if you played a low "Ab" and a high "Eb" there is a good chance you might hear these two notes in the key of "Ab" therefore "C" would sound like the 3rd which will tell you that you have modulated to the key of "Ab". Whether you stay in the original key of "C" or if you modulate will depend on the individual. Depending on the note combination and the octave they are in you may or may not modulate. But, if you find you never modulate then there is a problem because all two note combinations are not usually heard in the key of "C" though it is theoretically possible. After you have found the key you are in by listening to the "C" note your singing or hearing, then listen to the two notes as you would with the one note ear training to figure out the pitches.

For singing you should work on the 2, 3, and 4 note part singing found in this book. Keep in mind that it is possible to modulate within these example too. This will again depend on the individual; there is no right or wrong answer when it comes to whether you modulate or not. You can either play the other voices as you sing or you can use the midifiles found on the muse-eek website at www.muse-eek.com

It's important to realize that if you follow the steps I've outlined you can greatly change your perception and accuracy when it comes to pitch recognition and the ability to sing melodies. Naturally, some people progress very quickly with this method while for some people it can take years. The important thing is to do the method properly and with dedication, and over time your pitch recognition and singing ability will match anyone else's.

Exercise 1

Directions for Singing:
Beginning Student
1. Sing melody using solfeggio while playing a C Major Chord
Advanced Student
1. Sing melody using solfeggio with no accompaniment

Directions for Reading:
All Students
1. Sight read as written and 8va

Exercise 2

Directions for Singing:
Beginning Student
1. Sing melody using solfeggio while playing a C Major Chord
Advanced Student
1. Sing melody using solfeggio with no accompaniment

Directions for Reading:
All Students
1. Sight read as written and 8va

Exercise 3

Directions for Singing:
Beginning Student
1. Sing melody using solfeggio while playing a C Major Chord
Advanced Student
1. Sing melody using solfeggio with no accompaniment

Directions for Reading:
All Students
1. Sight read as written and 8va

Exercise 4

Directions for Singing:
Beginning Student
1. Sing melody using solfeggio while playing a C Major Chord
Advanced Student
1. Sing melody using solfeggio with no accompaniment

Directions for Reading:
All Students
1. Sight read as written and 8va

Exercise 5

Directions:
Advanced Students
1. Sing top melody using solfeggio while playing bottom part
2. Sing bottom melody using solfeggio while playing top part

Directions for reading for piano or guitar
Advanced Students
1. Sight read both parts as written and 8va

Exercise 6

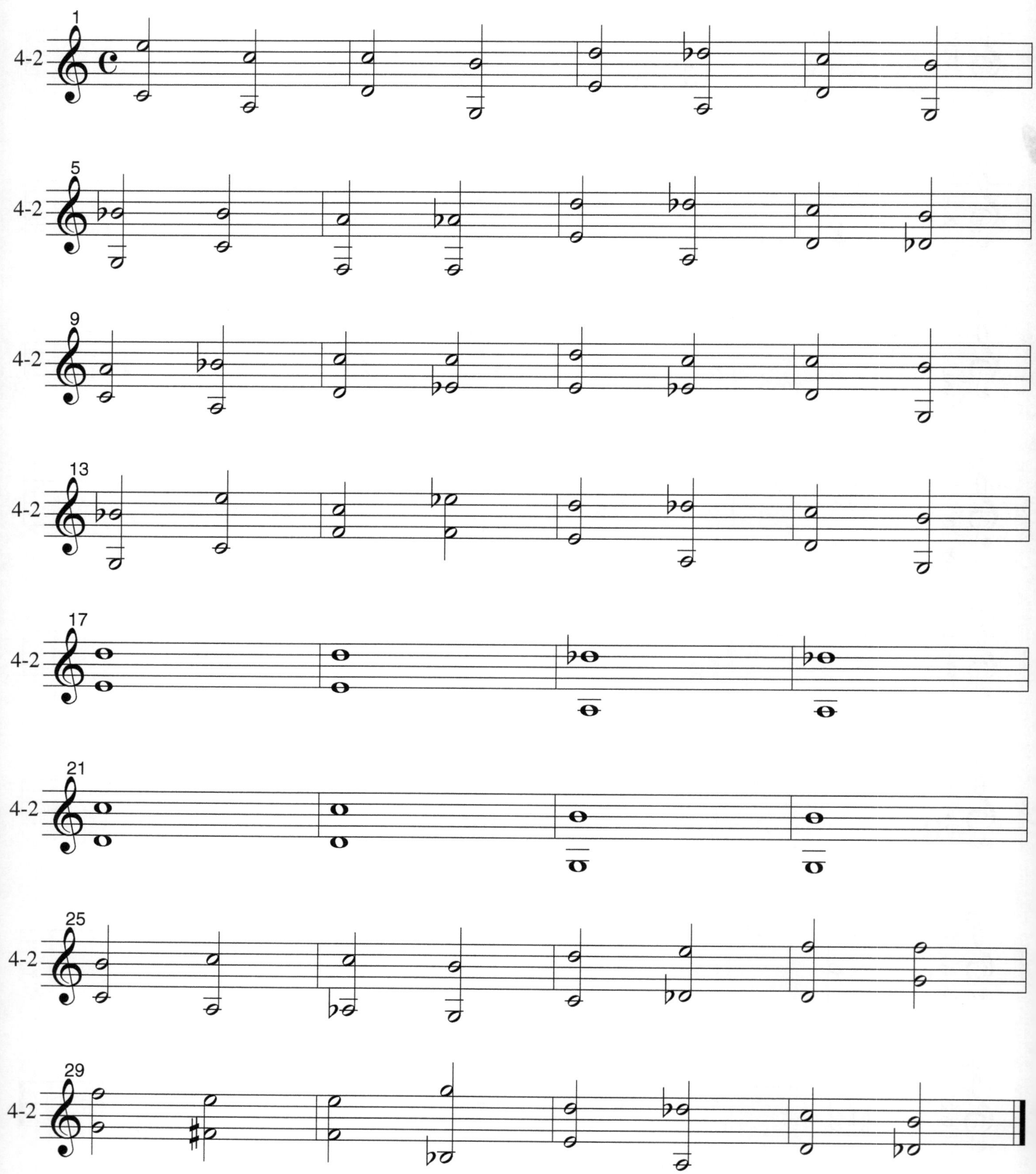

Directions for singing:
Advanced Students
1. Sing top melody using solfeggio while playing bottom part
2. Sing bottom melody using solfeggio while playing top part

Directions for reading for piano or guitar
Advanced Students
1. Sight read both parts as written and 8va

Exercise 7

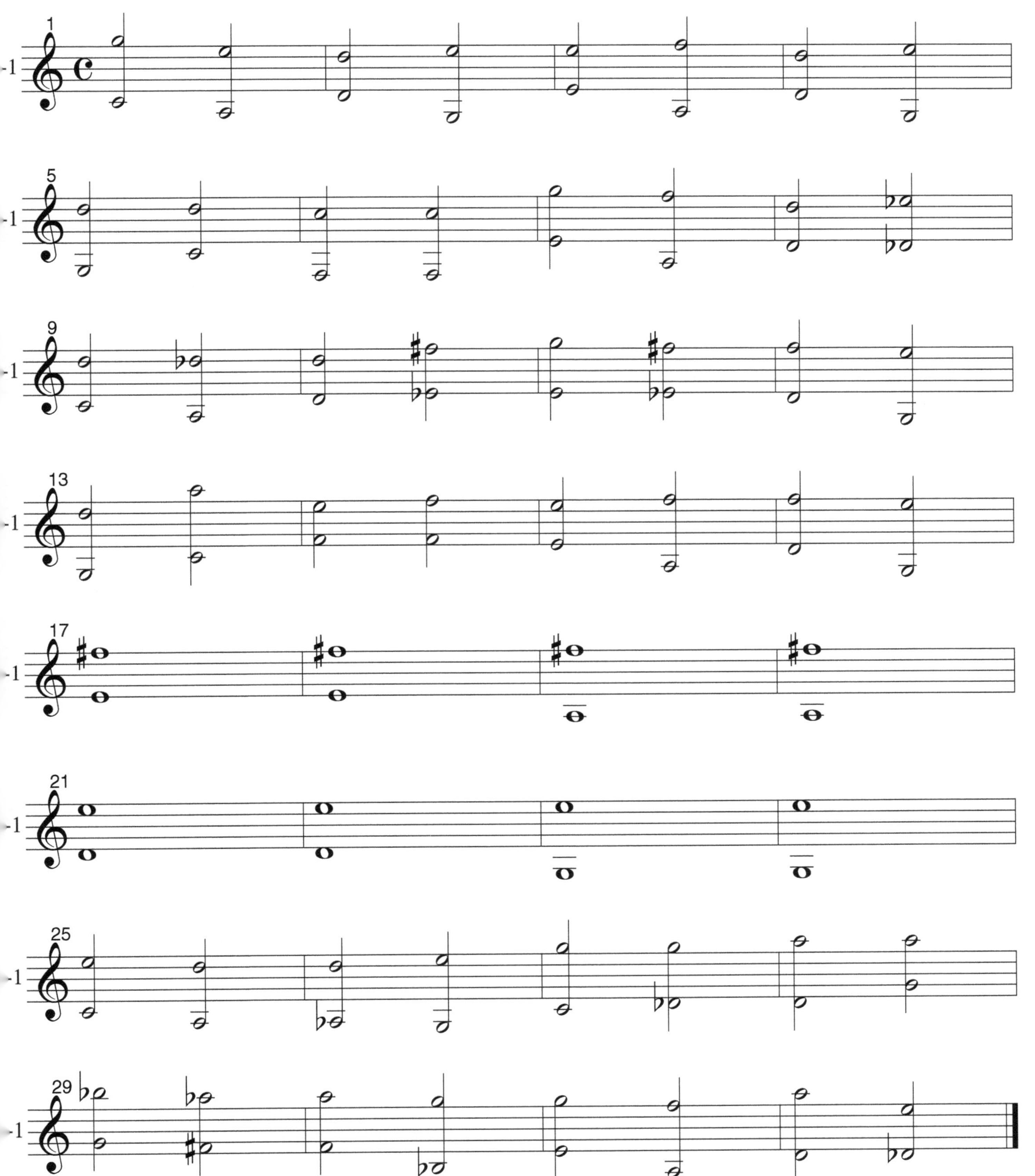

Directions for singing:
Advanced Students

1. Sing top melody using solfeggio while playing bottom part
2. Sing bottom melody using solfeggio while playing top part

Directions for reading for piano or guitar
Advanced Students

1. Sight read both parts as written and 8va

Exercise 8

Directionsfor singing:
Advanced Students
1. Sing top melody using solfeggio while playing bottom two parts
2. Sing middle melody using solfeggio while playing top and bottom parts
2. Sing bottom melody using solfeggio while playing upper two parts

Directions for reading for piano or guit
Advanced Students
1. Sight read all parts as written and 8

Exercise 9

Directions for singing:
Advanced Students
1. Sing top melody using solfeggio while playing bottom two parts
2. Sing middle melody using solfeggio while playing top and bottom parts
2. Sing bottom melody using solfeggio while playing upper two parts

Directions for reading for piano or guitar
Advanced Students
1. Sight read all parts as written and 8va

Exercise 10

Directions:
Advanced Students
1. Sing top melody using solfeggio while playing bottom three parts
2. Sing 2nd voice using solfeggio while playing other voices
3. Sing 3nd voice using solfeggio while playing other voices
4. Sing bottom voice using solfeggio while playing upper three parts

Directions for reading for piano or guitar
Advanced Students
1. Sight read all parts as written and 8va

Exercise 11

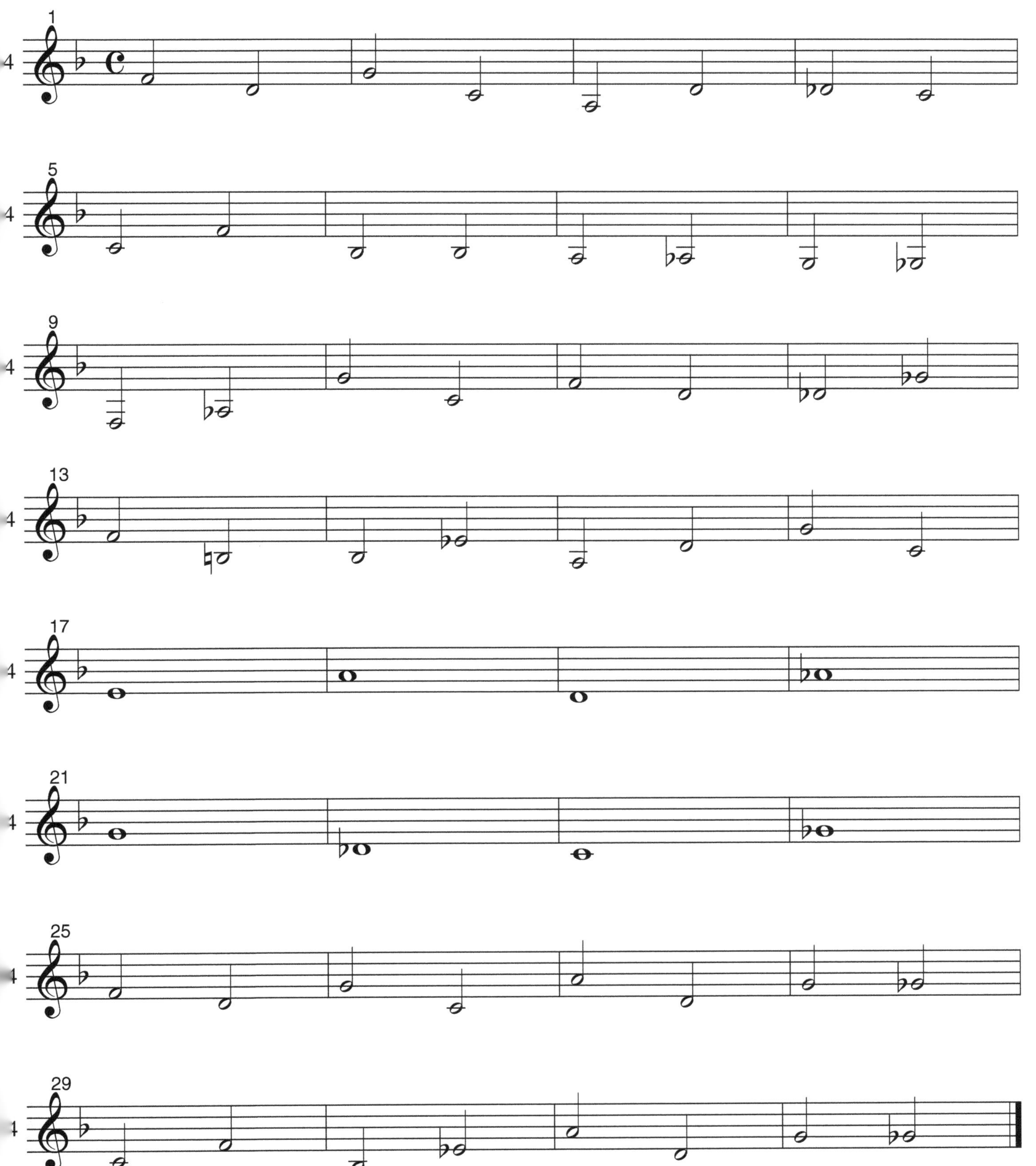

Directions for Singing:
Beginning Student
1. Sing melody using solfeggio while playing a F Major Chord
Advanced Student
1. Sing melody using solfeggio with no accompaniment

Directions for Reading:
All Students
1. Sight read as written and 8va

Exercise 12

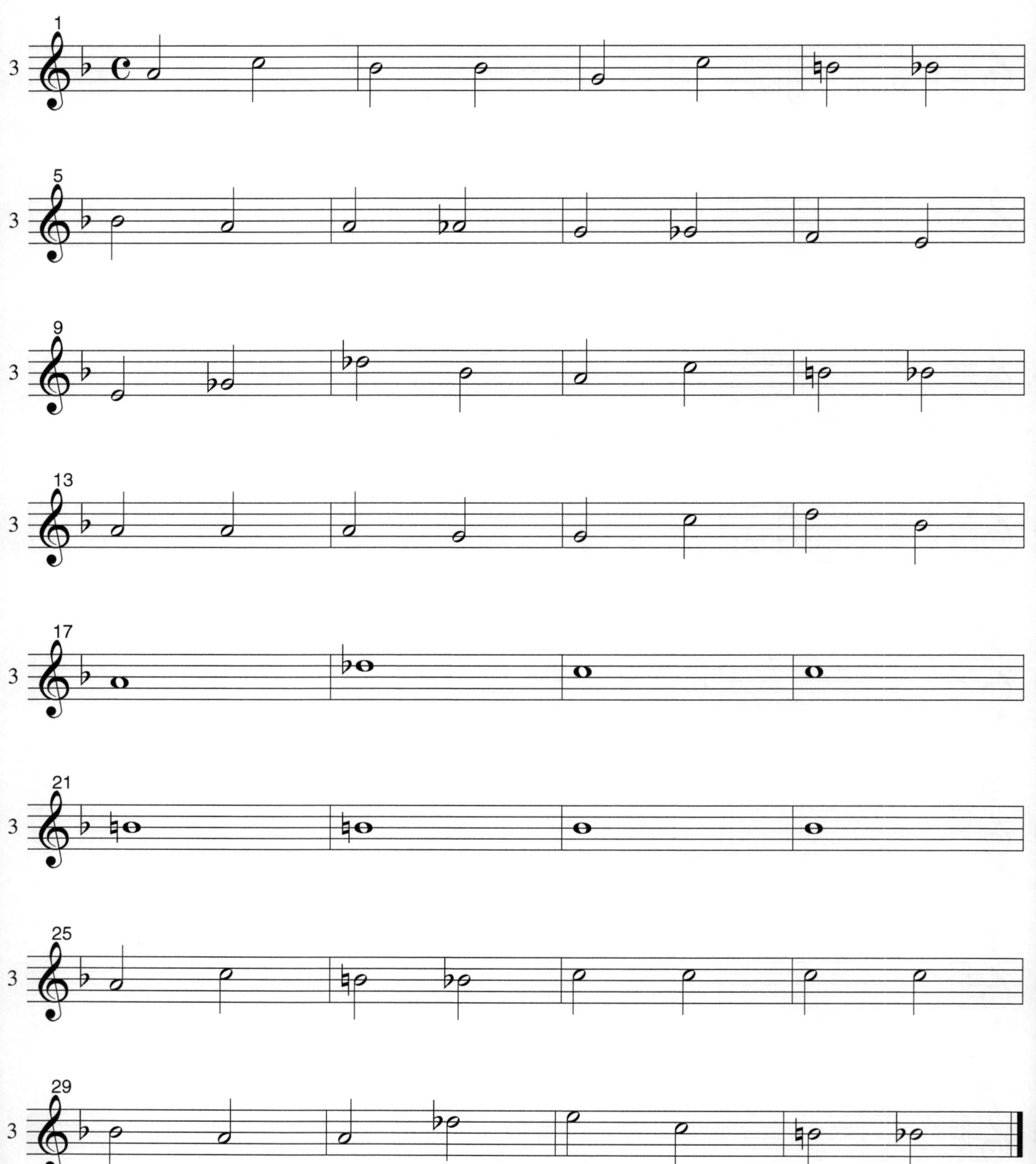

Directions for Singing:
Beginning Student
1. Sing melody using solfeggio while playing a F Major Chord
Advanced Student
1. Sing melody using solfeggio with no accompaniment

Directions for Reading:
All Students
1. Sigh tread as written and 8va

Exercise 13

Directions for Singing:
Beginning Student
1. Sing melody using solfeggio while playing a F Major Chord
Advanced Student
1. Sing melody using solfeggio with no accompaniment

Directions for Reading:
All Students
1. Sight read as written and 8va

Exercise 14

Directions for Singing:
Beginning Student
1. Sing melody using solfeggio while playing a F Major Chord
Advanced Student
1. Sing melody using solfeggio with no accompaniment

Directions for Reading:
All Students
1. Sight read as written and 8va

Exercise 15

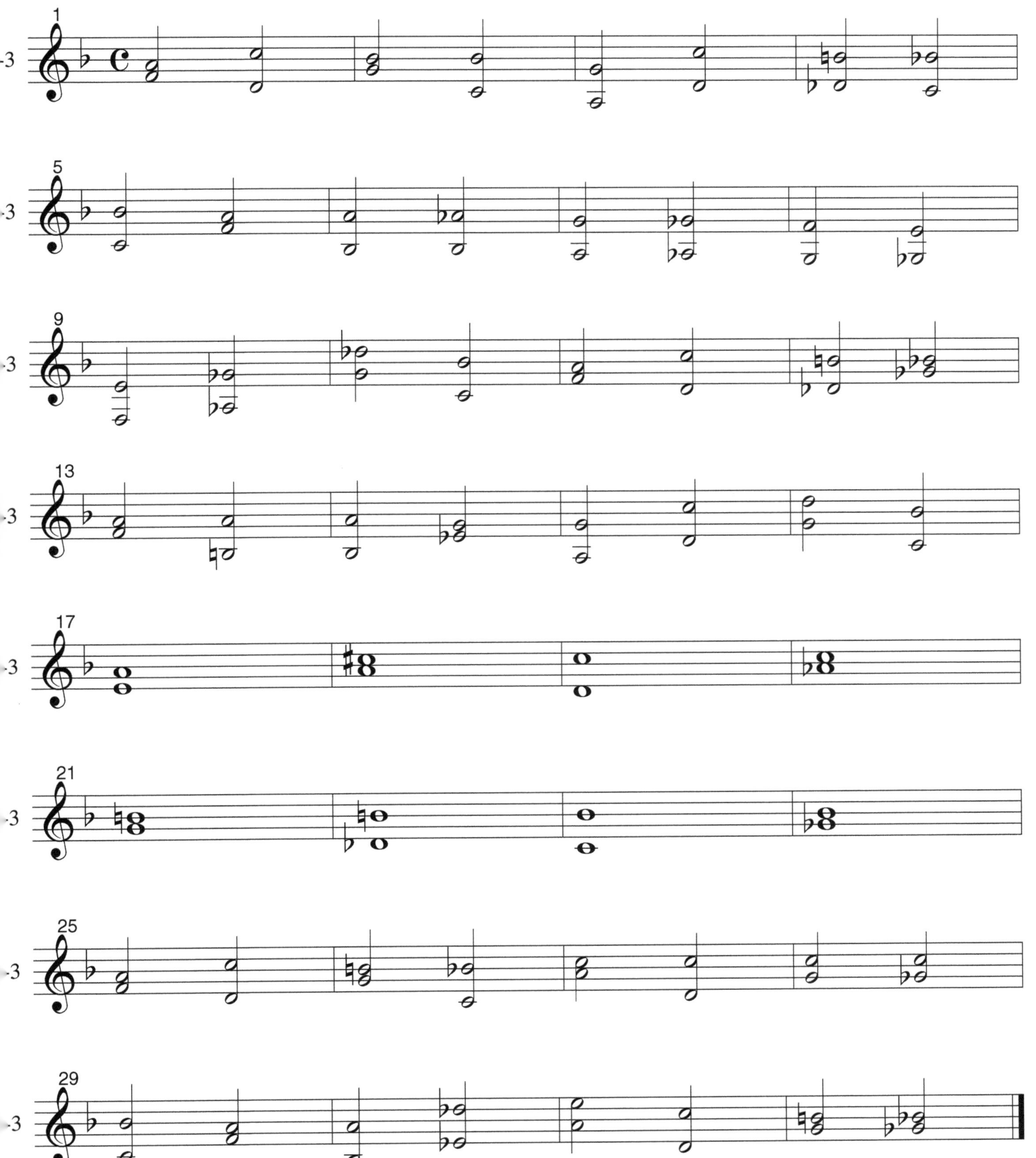

Directions:
Advanced Students
1. Sing top melody using solfeggio while playing bottom part
2. Sing bottom melody using solfeggio while playing top part

Directions for reading for piano or guitar
Advanced Students
1. Sight read both parts as written and 8va

Exercise 16

Directions for singing:
Advanced Students
1. Sing top melody using solfeggio while playing bottom part
2. Sing bottom melody using solfeggio while playing top part

Directions for reading for piano or guitar
Advanced Students
1. Sight read both parts as written and 8va

Exercise 17

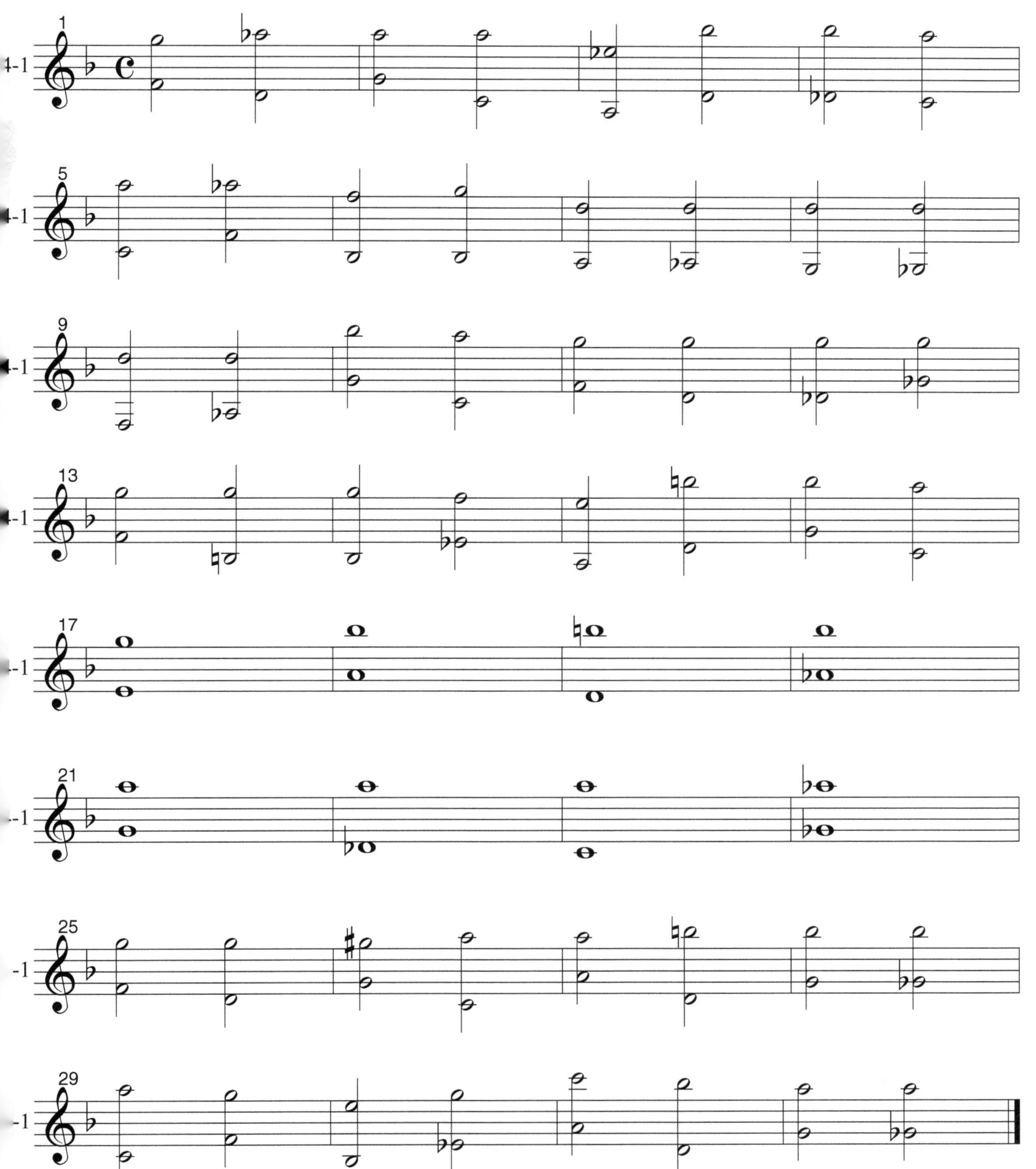

Directions for singing:
Advanced Students
1. Sing top melody using solfeggio while playing bottom part
2. Sing bottom melody using solfeggio while playing top part

Directions for reading for piano or guitar
Advanced Students
1. Sight read both parts as written and 8va

Exercise 18

Directionsfor singing:
Advanced Students

1. Sing top melody using solfeggio while playing bottom two parts
2. Sing middle melody using solfeggio while playing top and bottom parts
2. Sing bottom melody using solfeggio while playing upper two parts

Directions for reading for piano or guit
Advanced Students

1. Sight read all parts as written and 8v

Exercise 19

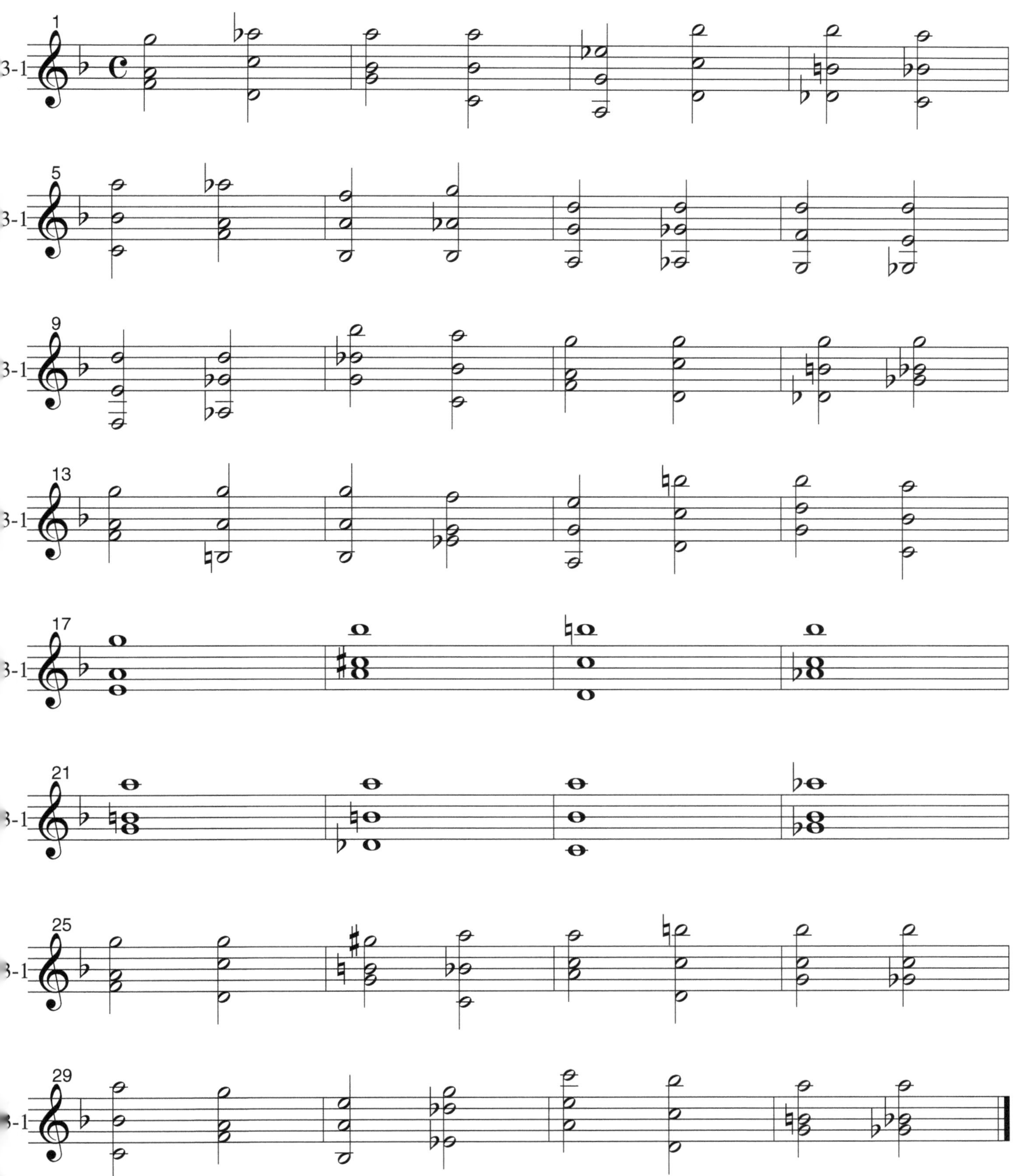

Directionsfor singing:
Advanced Students

1. Sing top melody using solfeggio while playing bottom two parts
2. Sing middle melody using solfeggio while playing top and bottom parts
2. Sing bottom melody using solfeggio while playing upper two parts

Directions for reading for piano or guitar
Advanced Students

1. Sight read all parts as written and 8va

Exercise 20

Directions:
Advanced Students
1. Sing top melody using solfeggio while playing bottom three parts
2. Sing 2nd voice using solfeggio while playing other voices
3. Sing 3nd voice using solfeggio while playing other voices
4. Sing bottom voice using solfeggio while playing upper three parts

Directions for reading for piano or guitar
Advanced Students
1. Sight read all parts as written and 8va

Exercise 21

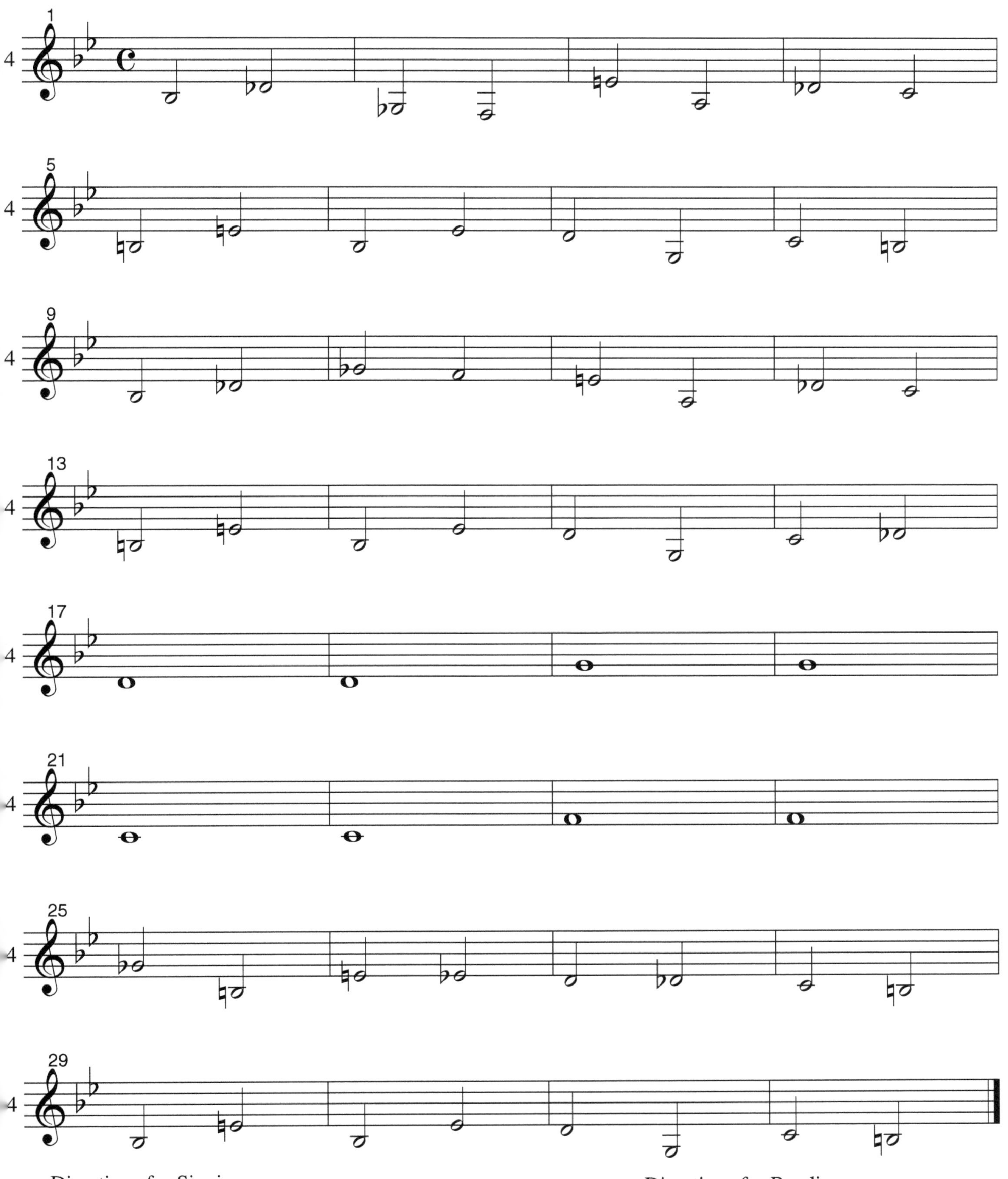

Directions for Singing:
Beginning Student
1. Sing melody using solfeggio while playing a F Major Chord
Advanced Student
1. Sing melody using solfeggio with no accompaniment

Directions for Reading:
All Students
1. Sight read as written and 8va

Exercise 22

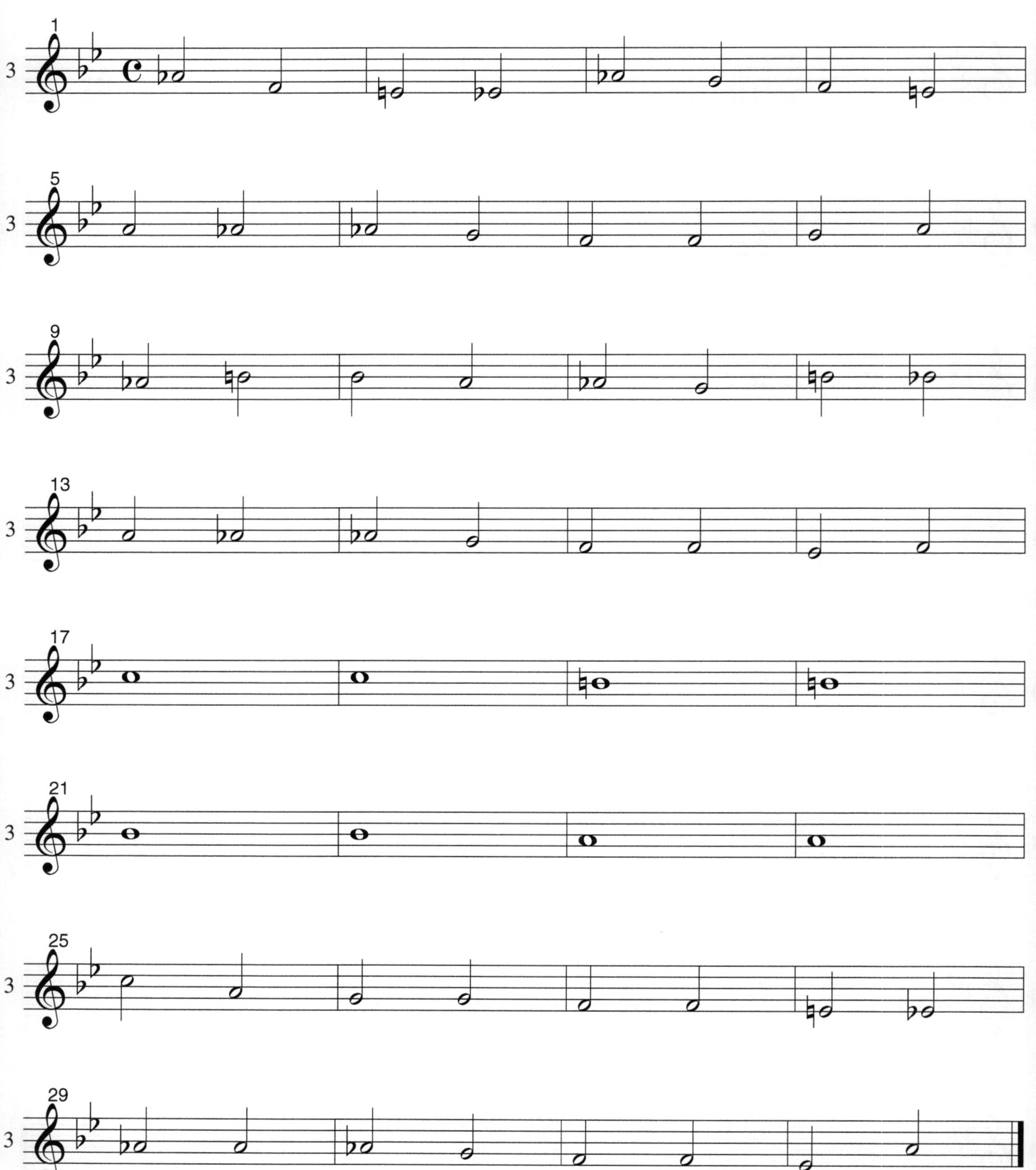

Directions for Singing:
Beginning Student
1. Sing melody using solfeggio while playing a Bb Major Chord
Advanced Student
1. Sing melody using solfeggio with no accompaniment

Directions for Reading:
All Students
1. Sight read as written and 8va

Exercise 23

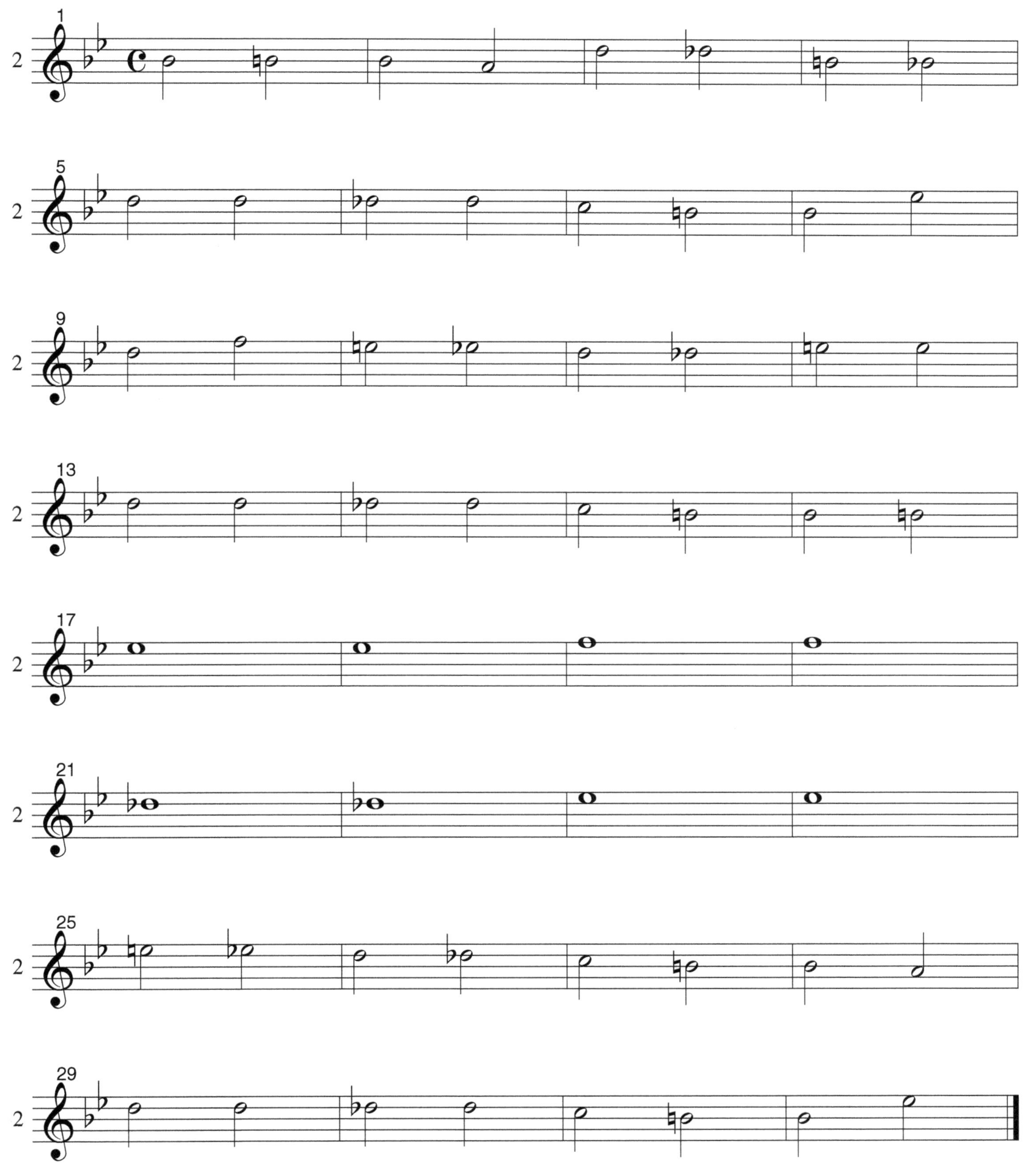

Directions for Singing:
Beginning Student
1. Sing melody using solfeggio while playing a Bb Major Chord
Advanced Student
1. Sing melody using solfeggio with no accompaniment

Directions for Reading:
All Students
1. Sightread as written and 8va

Exercise 24

Directions for Singing:
Beginning Student
1. Sing melody using solfeggio while playing a Bb Major Chord
Advanced Student
1. Sing melody using solfeggio with no accompaniment

Directions for Reading:
All Students
1. Sightread as written and 8va

Exercise 25

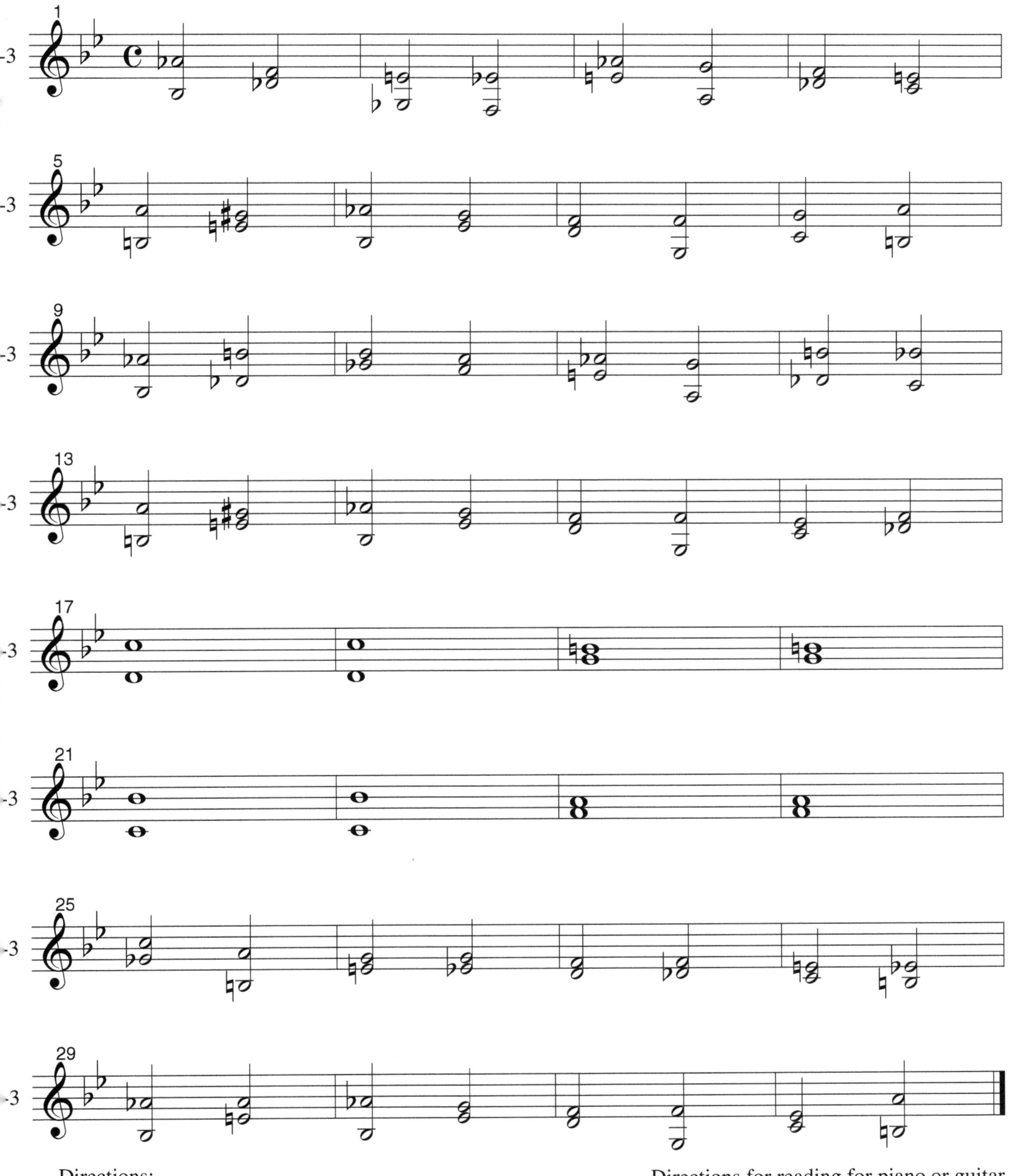

Directions:
Advanced Students
1. Sing top melody using solfeggio while playing bottom part
2. Sing bottom melody using solfeggio while playing top part

Directions for reading for piano or guitar
Advanced Students
1. Sightread both parts as written and 8va

Exercise 26

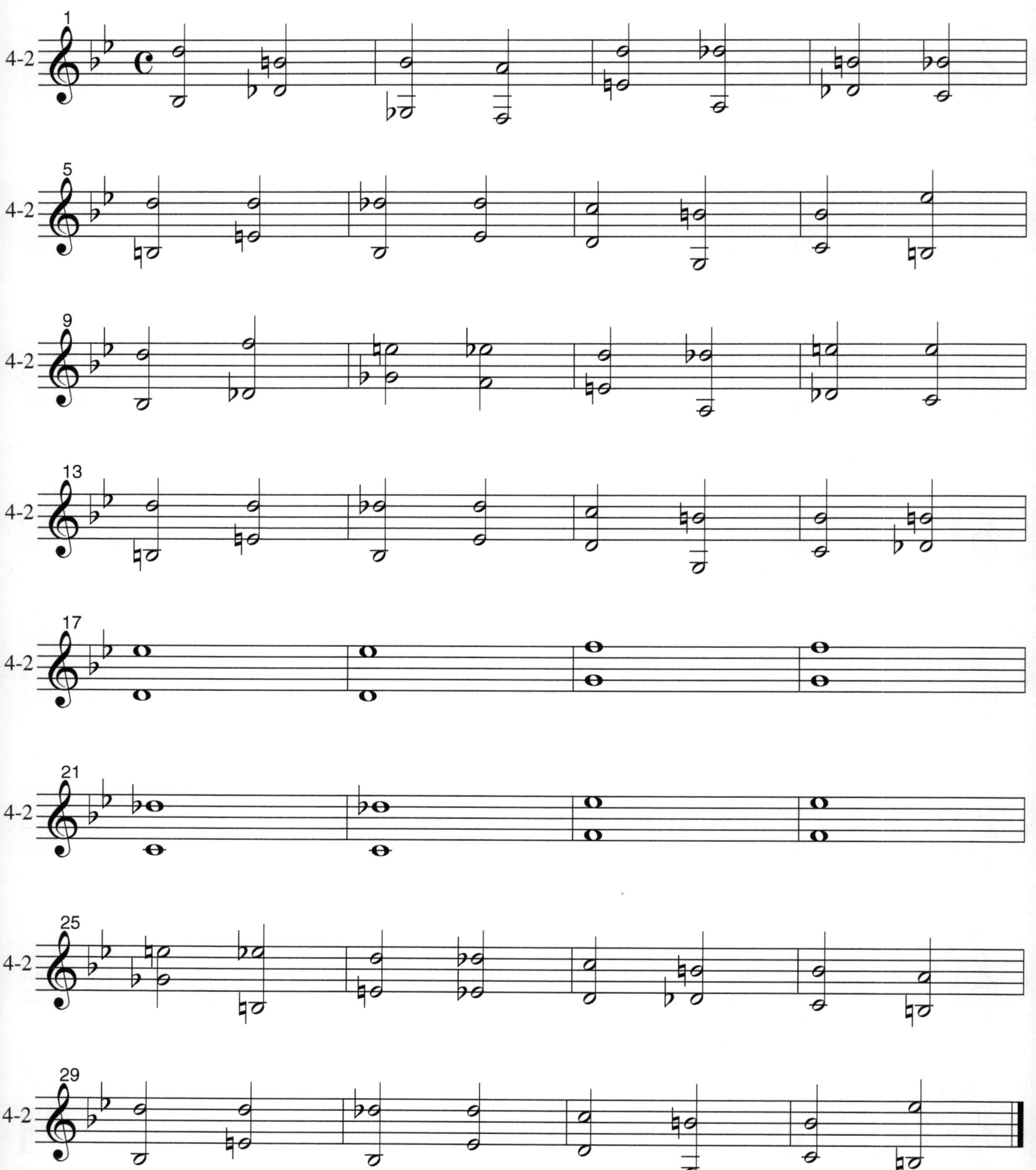

Directions for singing:
Advanced Students
1. Sing top melody using solfeggio while playing bottom part
2. Sing bottom melody using solfeggio while playing top part

Directions for reading for piano or guitar
Advanced Students
1. Sightread both parts as written and 8va

Exercise 27

Directions for singing:
Advanced Students
1. Sing top melody using solfeggio while playing bottom part
2. Sing bottom melody using solfeggio while playing top part

Directions for reading for piano or guitar
Advanced Students
1. Sightread both parts as written and 8va

Exercise 28

Directionsfor singing:
Advanced Students
1. Sing top melody using solfeggio while playing bottom two parts
2. Sing middle melody using solfeggio while playing top and bottom parts
2. Sing bottom melody using solfeggio while playing upper two parts

Directions for reading for piano or guit
Advanced Students
1. Sightread all parts as written and 8v

Exercise 29

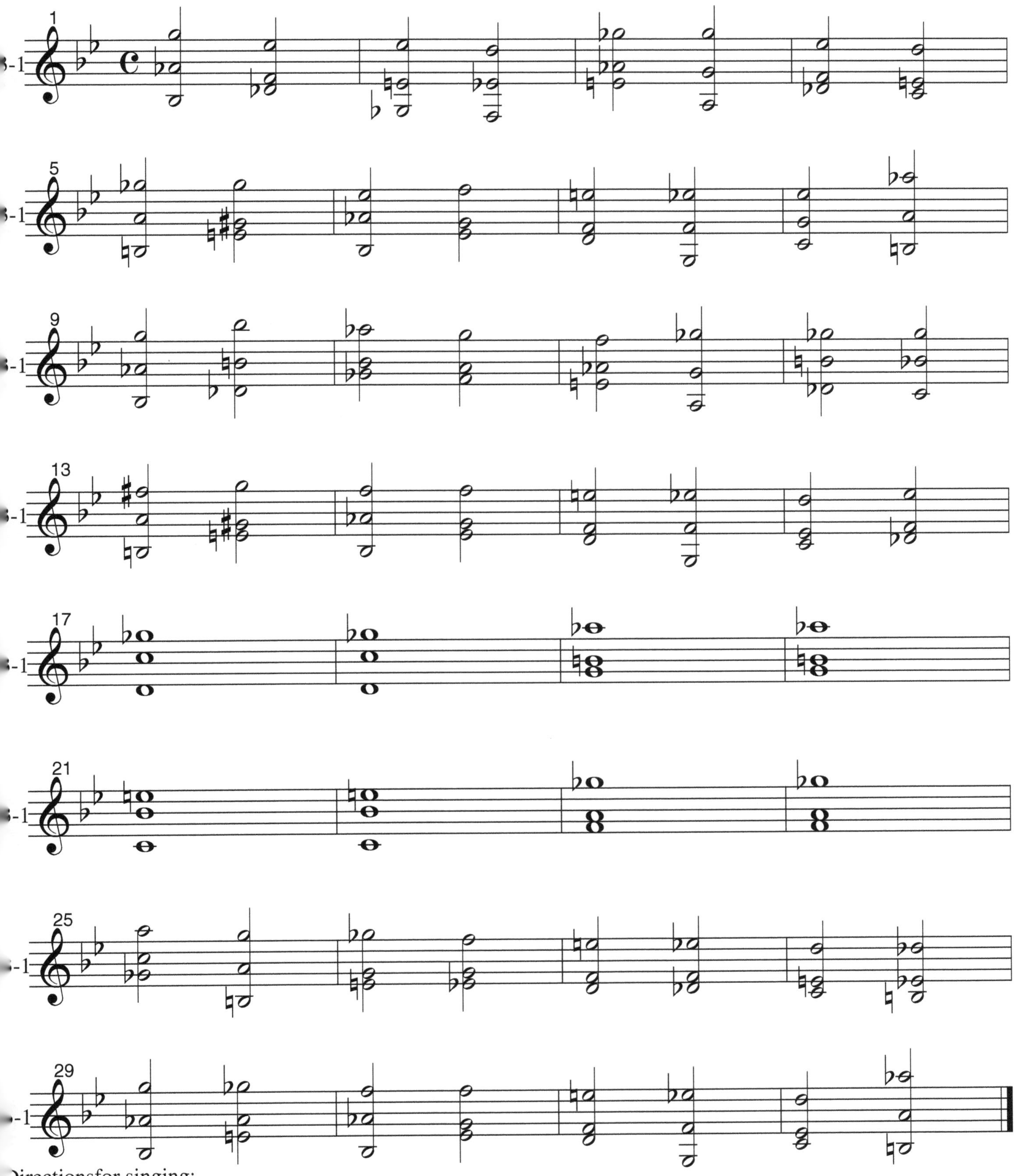

Directionsfor singing:
Advanced Students
1. Sing top melody using solfeggio while playing bottom two parts
2. Sing middle melody using solfeggio while playing top and bottom parts
3. Sing bottom melody using solfeggio while playing upper two parts

Directions for reading for piano or guitar
Advanced Students
1. Sightread all parts as written and 8va

Exercise 30

Directions:
Advanced Students
1. Sing top melody using solfeggio while playing bottom three parts
2. Sing 2nd voice using solfeggio while playing other voices
3. Sing 3nd voice using solfeggio while playing other voices
4. Sing bottom voice using solfeggio while playing upper three parts

Directions for reading for piano or guitar
Advanced Students
1. Sightread all parts as written and 8va

Exercise 31

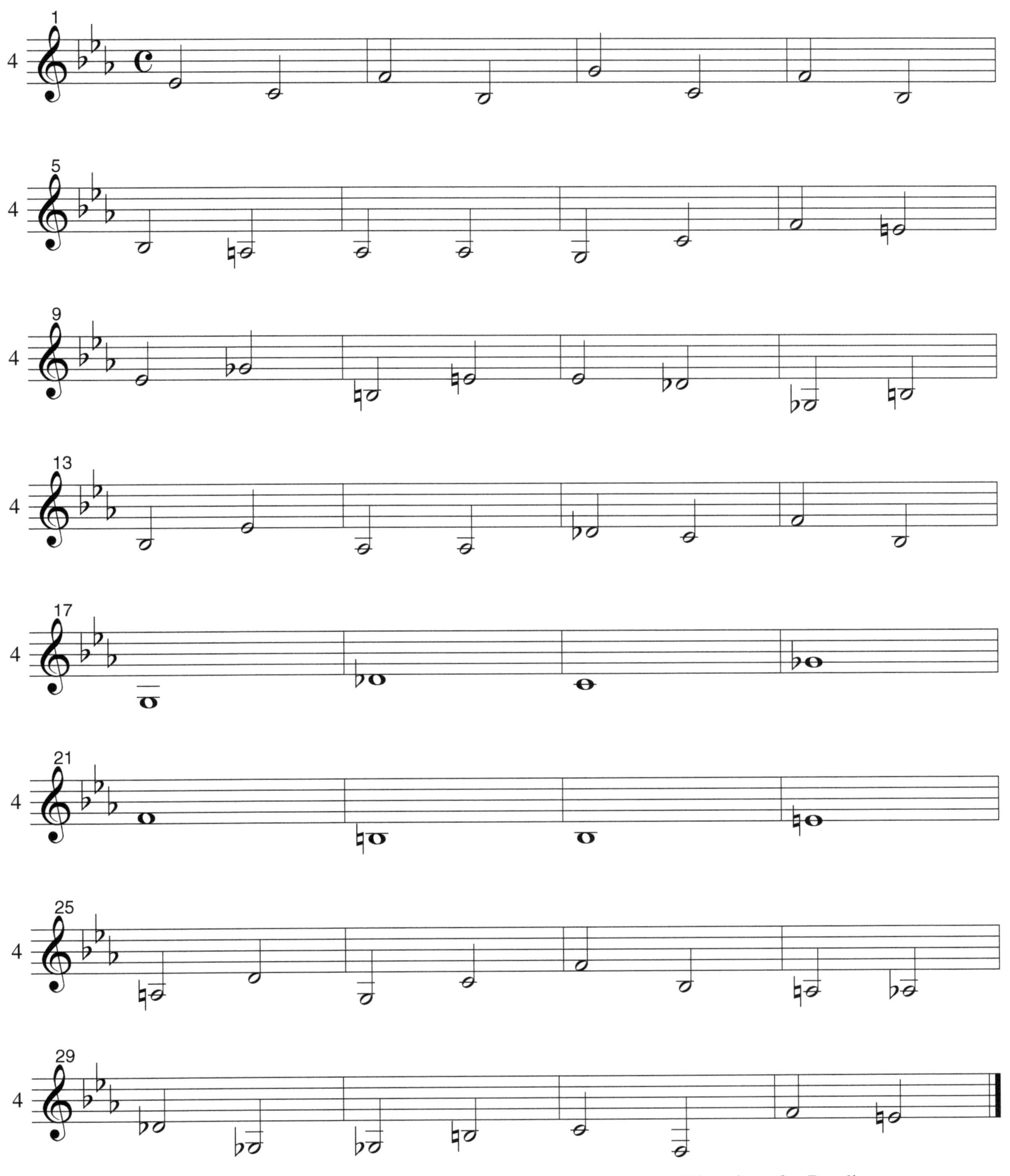

Directions for Singing:
Beginning Student
1. Sing melody using solfeggio while playing a Eb Major Chord
Advanced Student
1. Sing melody using solfeggio with no accompaniment

Directions for Reading:
All Students
1. Sight read as written and 8va

Exercise 32

Directions for Singing:
Beginning Student
1. Sing melody using solfeggio while playing a Eb Major Chord
Advanced Student
1. Sing melody using solfeggio with no accompaniment

Directions for Reading:
All Students
1. Sight read as written and 8va

Exercise 33

Directions for Singing:
Beginning Student
1. Sing melody using solfeggio while playing a Eb Major Chord
Advanced Student
1. Sing melody using solfeggio with no accompaniment

Directions for Reading:
All Students
1. Sight read as written and 8va

Exercise 34

Directions for Singing:
Beginning Student
1. Sing melody using solfeggio while playing a Eb Major Chord
Advanced Student
1. Sing melody using solfeggio with no accompaniment

Directions for Reading:
All Students
1. Sight read as written and 8va

Exercise 35

Directions:
Advanced Students
1. Sing top melody using solfeggio while playing bottom part
2. Sing bottom melody using solfeggio while playing top part

Directions for reading for piano or guitar
Advanced Students
1. Sight read both parts as written and 8va

Exercise 36

Directions for singing:
Advanced Students
1. Sing top melody using solfeggio while playing bottom part
2. Sing bottom melody using solfeggio while playing top part

Directions for reading for piano or guitar
Advanced Students
1. Sight read both parts as written and 8va

Exercise 37

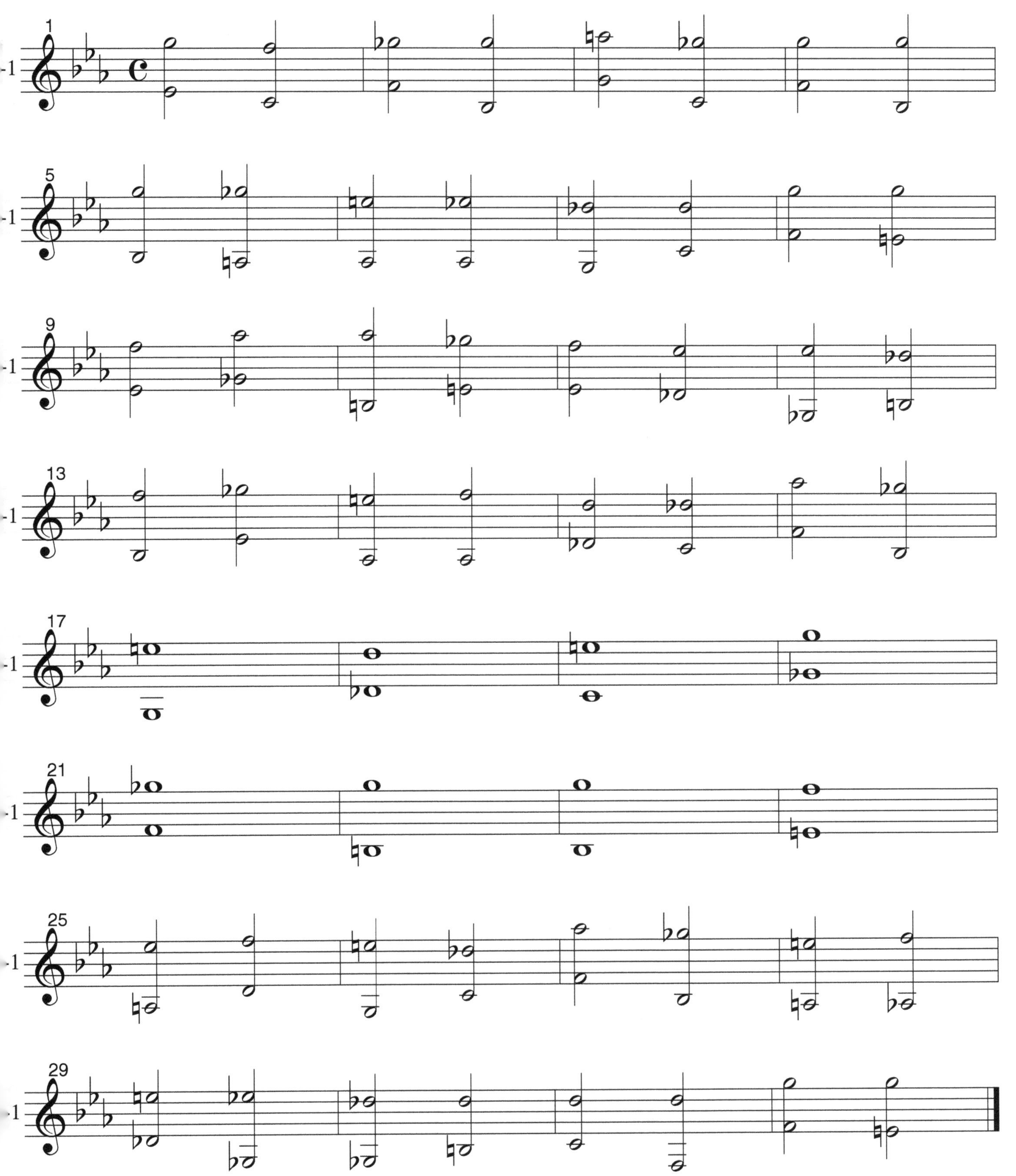

Directions for singing:
Advanced Students
1. Sing top melody using solfeggio while playing bottom part
2. Sing bottom melody using solfeggio while playing top part

Directions for reading for piano or guitar
Advanced Students
1. Sight read both parts as written and 8va

Exercise 38

Directions for singing:
Advanced Students
1. Sing top melody using solfeggio while playing bottom two parts
2. Sing middle melody using solfeggio while playing top and bottom parts
2. Sing bottom melody using solfeggio while playing upper two parts

Directions for reading for piano or guita
Advanced Students
1. Sight read all parts as written and 8v

Exercise 39

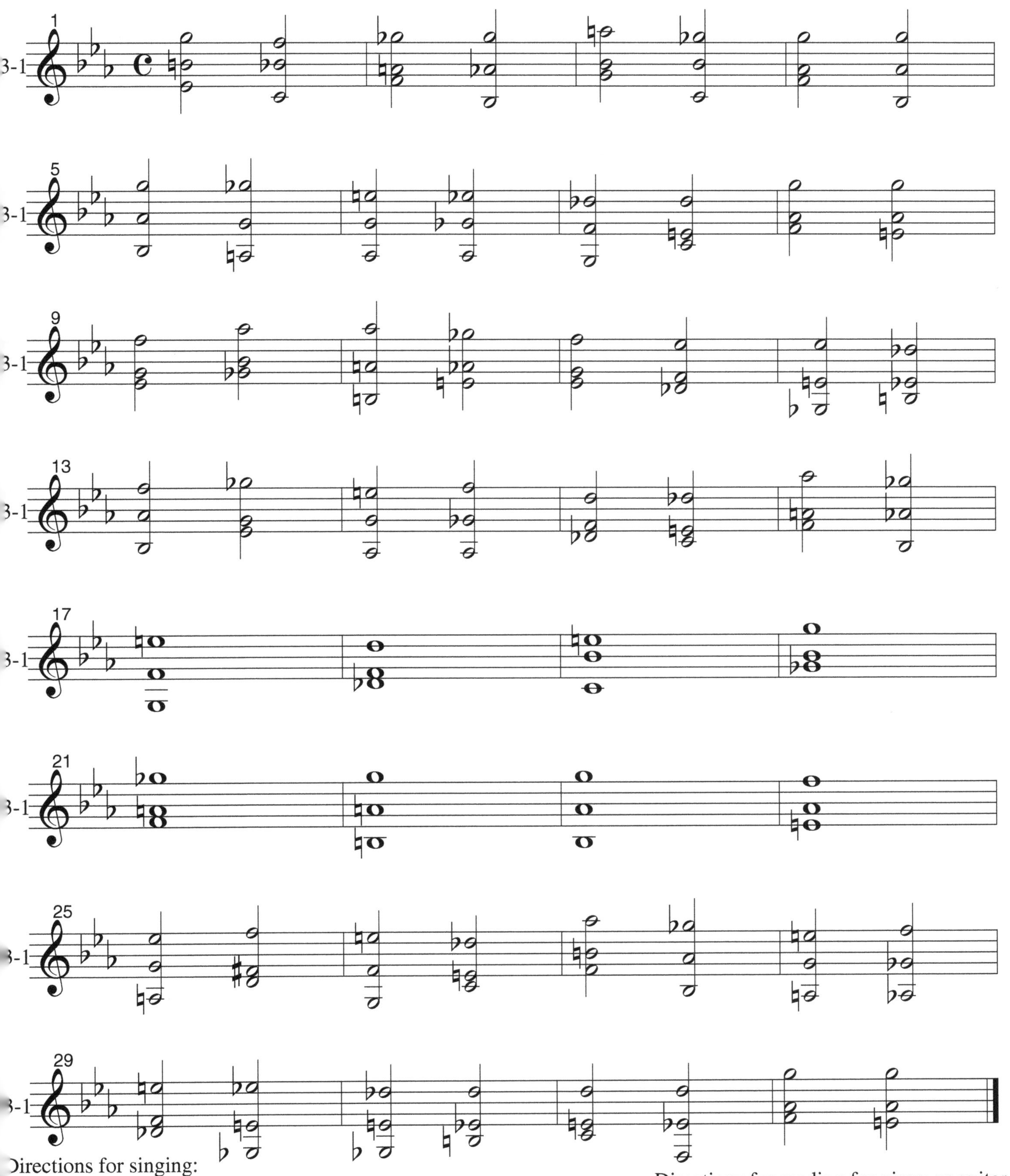

Directions for singing:
Advanced Students
1. Sing top melody using solfeggio while playing bottom two parts
2. Sing middle melody using solfeggio while playing top and bottom parts
3. Sing bottom melody using solfeggio while playing upper two parts

Directions for reading for piano or guitar
Advanced Students
1. Sight read all parts as written and 8va

Exercise 40

Directions:
Advanced Students
1. Sing top melody using solfeggio while playing bottom three parts
2. Sing 2nd voice using solfeggio while playing other voices
3. Sing 3nd voice using solfeggio while playing other voices
4. Sing bottom voice using solfeggio while playing upper three parts

Directions for reading for piano or guitar
Advanced Students
1. Sight read all parts as written and 8va

Exercise 41

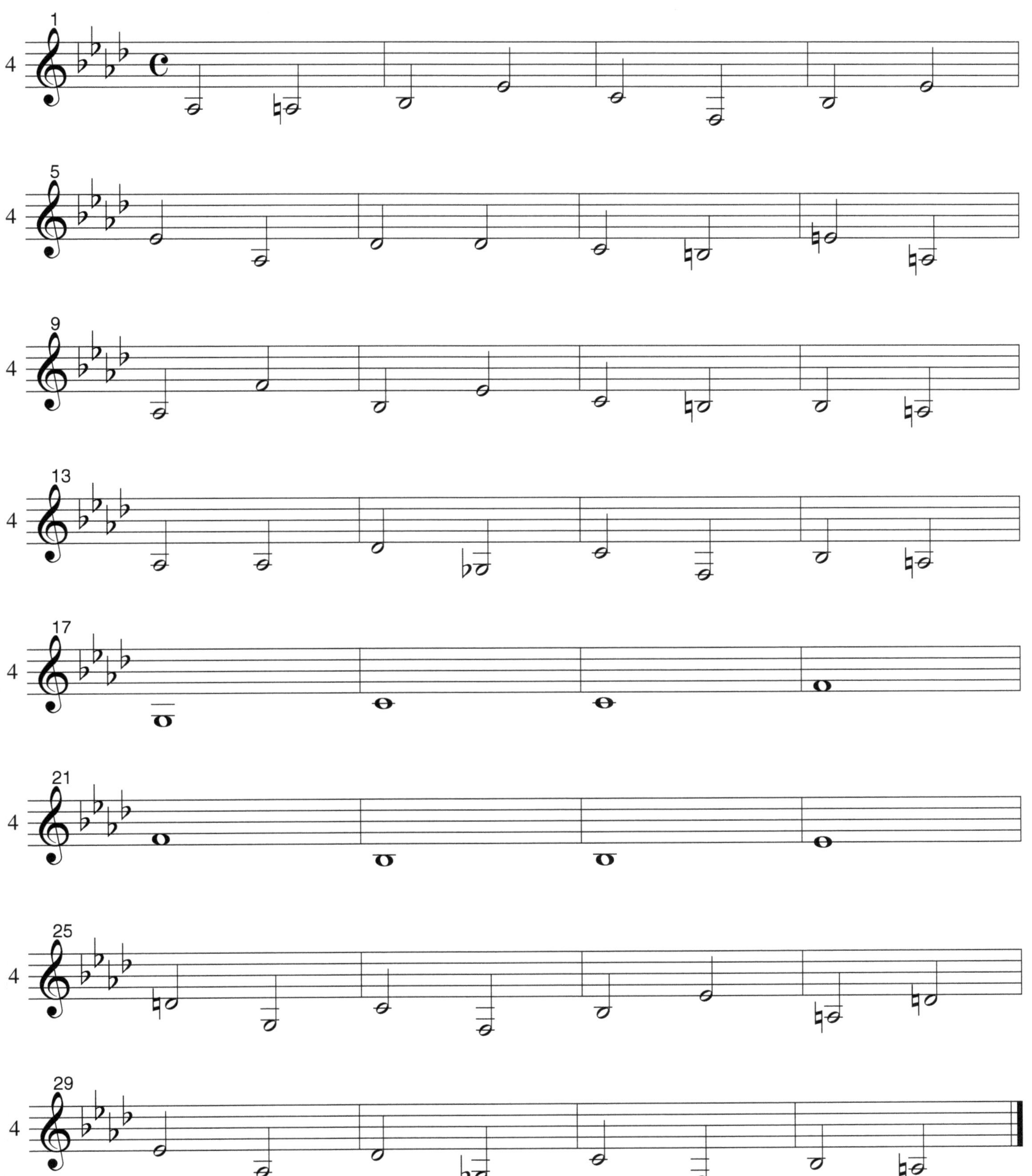

Directions for Singing:
Beginning Student
1. Sing melody using solfeggio while playing a C Major Chord
Advanced Student
1. Sing melody using solfeggio with no accompaniment

Directions for Reading:
All Students
1. Sight read as written and 8va

Exercise 42

Directions for Singing:
Beginning Student
1. Sing melody using solfeggio while playing a C Major Chord
Advanced Student
1. Sing melody using solfeggio with no accompaniment

Directions for Reading:
All Students
1. Sight read as written and 8va

Exercise 43

Directions for Singing:
Beginning Student
1. Sing melody using solfeggio while playing a C Major Chord
Advanced Student
1. Sing melody using solfeggio with no accompaniment

Directions for Reading:
All Students
1. Sight read as written and 8va

Exercise 44

Directions for Singing:
Beginning Student
1. Sing melody using solfeggio while playing a C Major Chord
Advanced Student
1. Sing melody using solfeggio with no accompaniment

Directions for Reading:
All Students
1. Sight read as written and 8va

Exercise 45

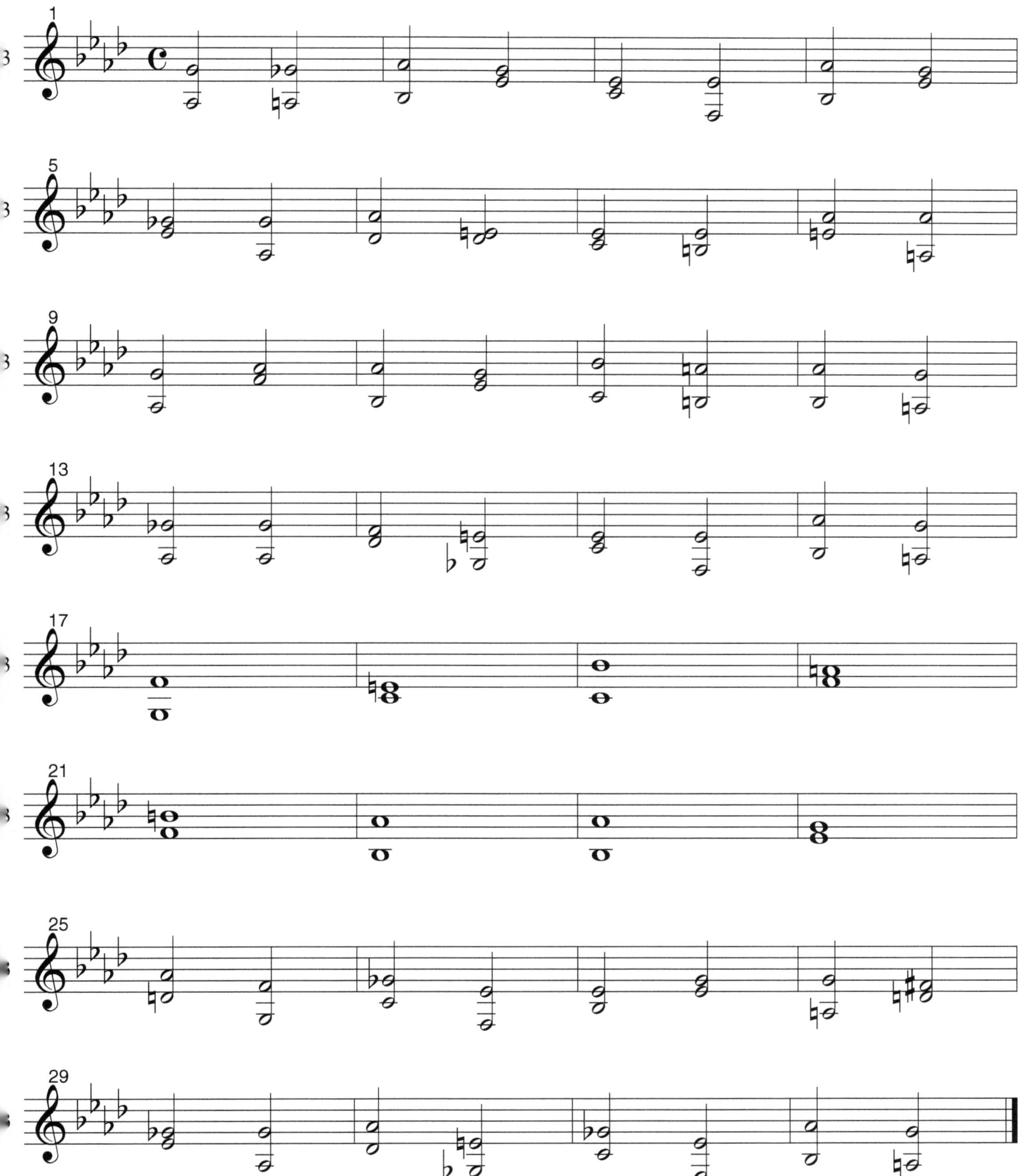

Directions:
Advanced Students
1. Sing top melody using solfeggio while playing bottom part
2. Sing bottom melody using solfeggio while playing top part

Directions for reading for piano or guitar
Advanced Students
1. Sight read both parts as written and 8va

Exercise 46

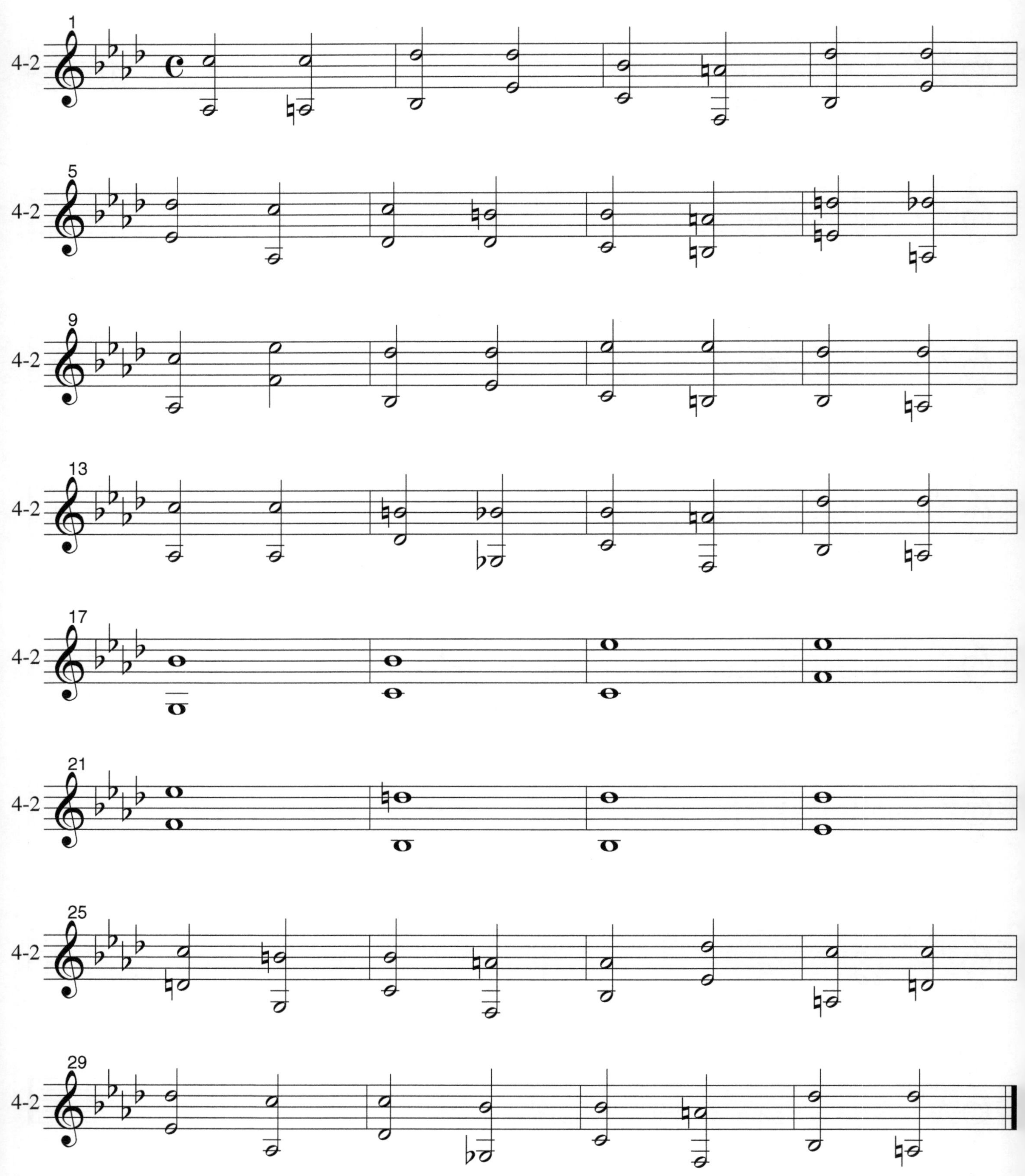

Directions for singing:
Advanced Students
1. Sing top melody using solfeggio while playing bottom part
2. Sing bottom melody using solfeggio while playing top part

Directions for reading for piano or guitar
Advanced Students
1. Sight read both parts as written and 8va

Exercise 47

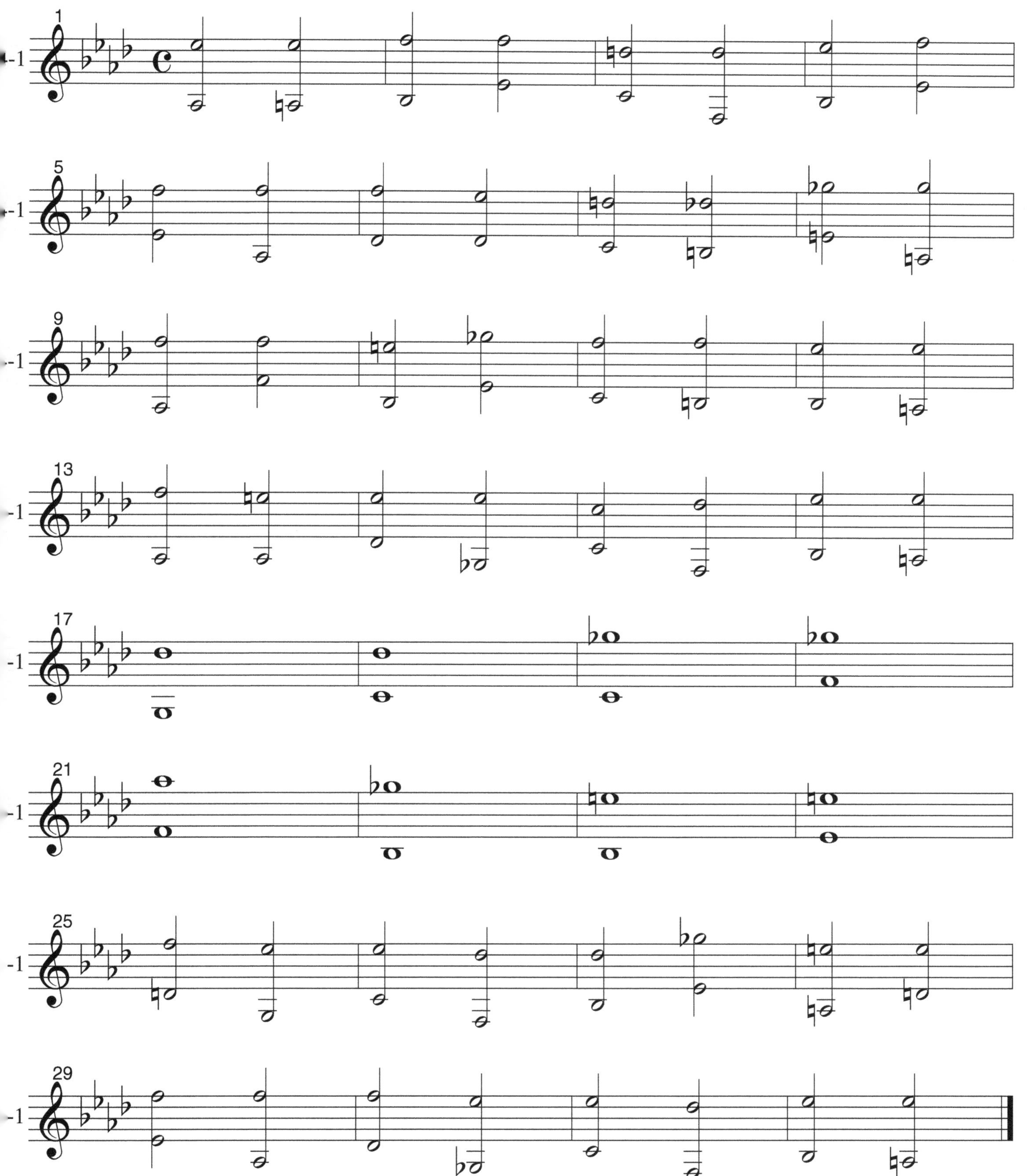

Directions for singing:
Advanced Students
1. Sing top melody using solfeggio while playing bottom part
2. Sing bottom melody using solfeggio while playing top part

Directions for reading for piano or guitar
Advanced Students
1. Sight read both parts as written and 8va

Exercise 48

Directionsfor singing:
Advanced Students
1. Sing top melody using solfeggio while playing bottom two parts
2. Sing middle melody using solfeggio while playing top and bottom parts
2. Sing bottom melody using solfeggio while playing upper two parts

Directions for reading for piano or guit
Advanced Students
1. Sight read all parts as written and 8

Exercise 49

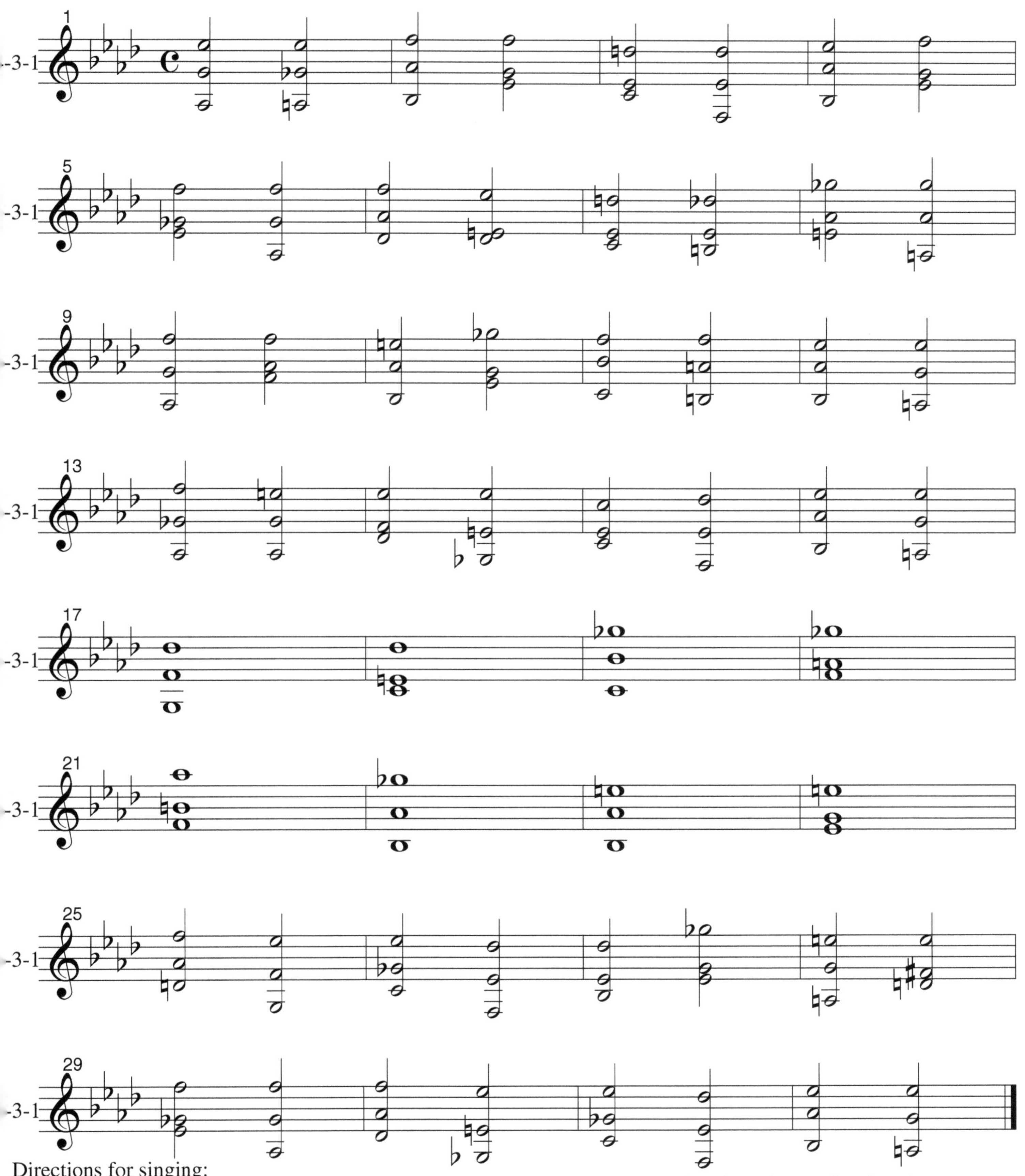

Directions for singing:
Advanced Students
1. Sing top melody using solfeggio while playing bottom two parts
2. Sing middle melody using solfeggio while playing top and bottom parts
2. Sing bottom melody using solfeggio while playing upper two parts

Directions for reading for piano or guitar
Advanced Students
1. Sight read all parts as written and 8va

Exercise 50

Directions:
Advanced Students
1. Sing top melody using solfeggio while playing bottom three parts
2. Sing 2nd voice using solfeggio while playing other voices
3. Sing 3nd voice using solfeggio while playing other voices
4. Sing bottom voice using solfeggio while playing upper three parts

Directions for reading for piano or guitar
Advanced Students
1. Sight read all parts as written and 8va

Exercise 51

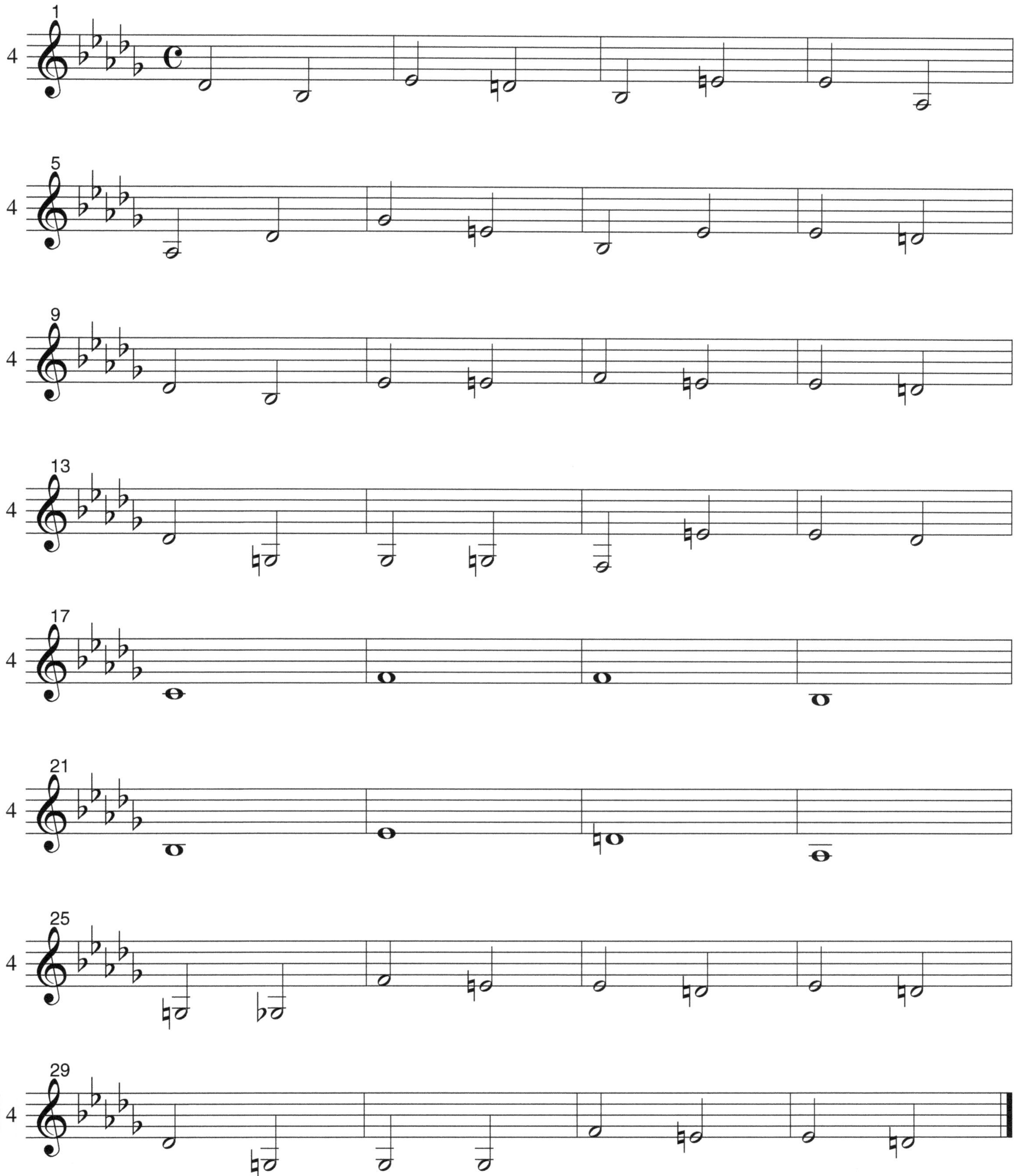

Directions for Singing:
Beginning Student
1. Sing melody using solfeggio while playing a Db Major Chord
Advanced Student
1. Sing melody using solfeggio with no accompaniment

Directions for Reading:
All Students
1. Sight read as written and 8va

Exercise 52

Directions for Singing:
Beginning Student
1. Sing melody using solfeggio while playing a Db Major Chord
Advanced Student
1. Sing melody using solfeggio with no accompaniment

Directions for Reading:
All Students
1. Sight read as written and 8va

Exercise 53

Directions for Singing:
Beginning Student
1. Sing melody using solfeggio while playing a Db Major Chord
Advanced Student
1. Sing melody using solfeggio with no accompaniment

Directions for Reading:
All Students
1. Sight read as written and 8va

Exercise 54

Directions for Singing:
Beginning Student
1. Sing melody using solfeggio while playing a Db Major Chord
Advanced Student
1. Sing melody using solfeggio with no accompaniment

Directions for Reading:
All Students
1. Sight read as written and 8va

Exercise 55

Directions:
Advanced Students
1. Sing top melody using solfeggio while playing bottom part
2. Sing bottom melody using solfeggio while playing top part

Directions for reading for piano or guitar
Advanced Students
1. Sight read both parts as written and 8va

Exercise 56

Directions for singing:
Advanced Students
1. Sing top melody using solfeggio while playing bottom part
2. Sing bottom melody using solfeggio while playing top part

Directions for reading for piano or guitar
Advanced Students
1. Sight read both parts as written and 8va

Exercise 57

Directionsfor singing:
Advanced Students
1. Sing top melody using solfeggio while playing bottom two parts
2. Sing middle melody using solfeggio while playing top and bottom parts
2. Sing bottom melody using solfeggio while playing upper two parts

Directions for reading for piano or guitar
Advanced Students
1. Sight read all parts as written and 8va

Exercise 58

Directionsfor singing:
Advanced Students
1. Sing top melody using solfeggio while playing bottom two parts
2. Sing middle melody using solfeggio while playing top and bottom parts
2. Sing bottom melody using solfeggio while playing upper two parts

Directions for reading for piano or guita
Advanced Students
1. Sight read all parts as written and 8v.

Exercise 59

Directions for singing:
Advanced Students
1. Sing top melody using solfeggio while playing bottom two parts
2. Sing middle melody using solfeggio while playing top and bottom parts
2. Sing bottom melody using solfeggio while playing upper two parts

Directions for reading for piano or guitar
Advanced Students
1. Sight read all parts as written and 8va

Exercise 60

Directions:
Advanced Students
1. Sing top melody using solfeggio while playing bottom three parts
2. Sing 2nd voice using solfeggio while playing other voices
3. Sing 3nd voice using solfeggio while playing other voices
4. Sing bottom voice using solfeggio while playing upper three parts

Directions for reading for piano or guitar
Advanced Students
1. Sight read all parts as written and 8va

Exercise 61

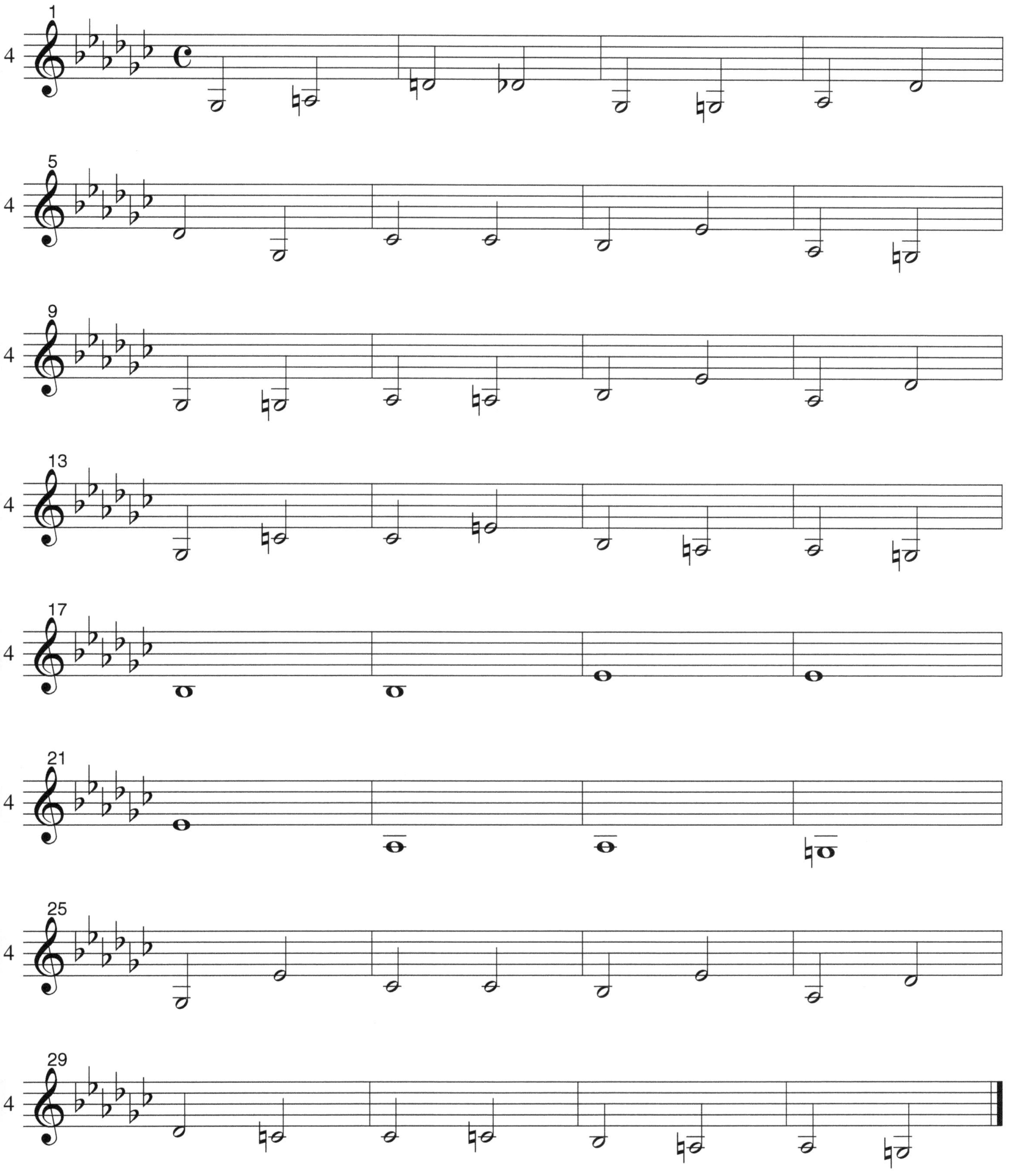

Directions for Singing:
Beginning Student
1. Sing melody using solfeggio while playing a Gb Major Chord
Advanced Student
1. Sing melody using solfeggio with no accompaniment

Directions for Reading:
All Students
1. Sight read as written and 8va

Exercise 62

Directions for Singing:
Beginning Student
1. Sing melody using solfeggio while playing a Gb Major Chord
Advanced Student
1. Sing melody using solfeggio with no accompaniment

Directions for Reading:
All Students
1. Sight read as written and 8va

Exercise 63

Directions for Singing:
Beginning Student
1. Sing melody using solfeggio while playing a Gb Major Chord
Advanced Student
1. Sing melody using solfeggio with no accompaniment

Directions for Reading:
All Students
1. Sight read as written and 8va

Exercise 64

Directions for Singing:
Beginning Student
1. Sing melody using solfeggio while playing a Gb Major Chord
Advanced Student
1. Sing melody using solfeggio with no accompaniment

Directions for Reading:
All Students
1. Sight read as written and 8va

Exercise 65

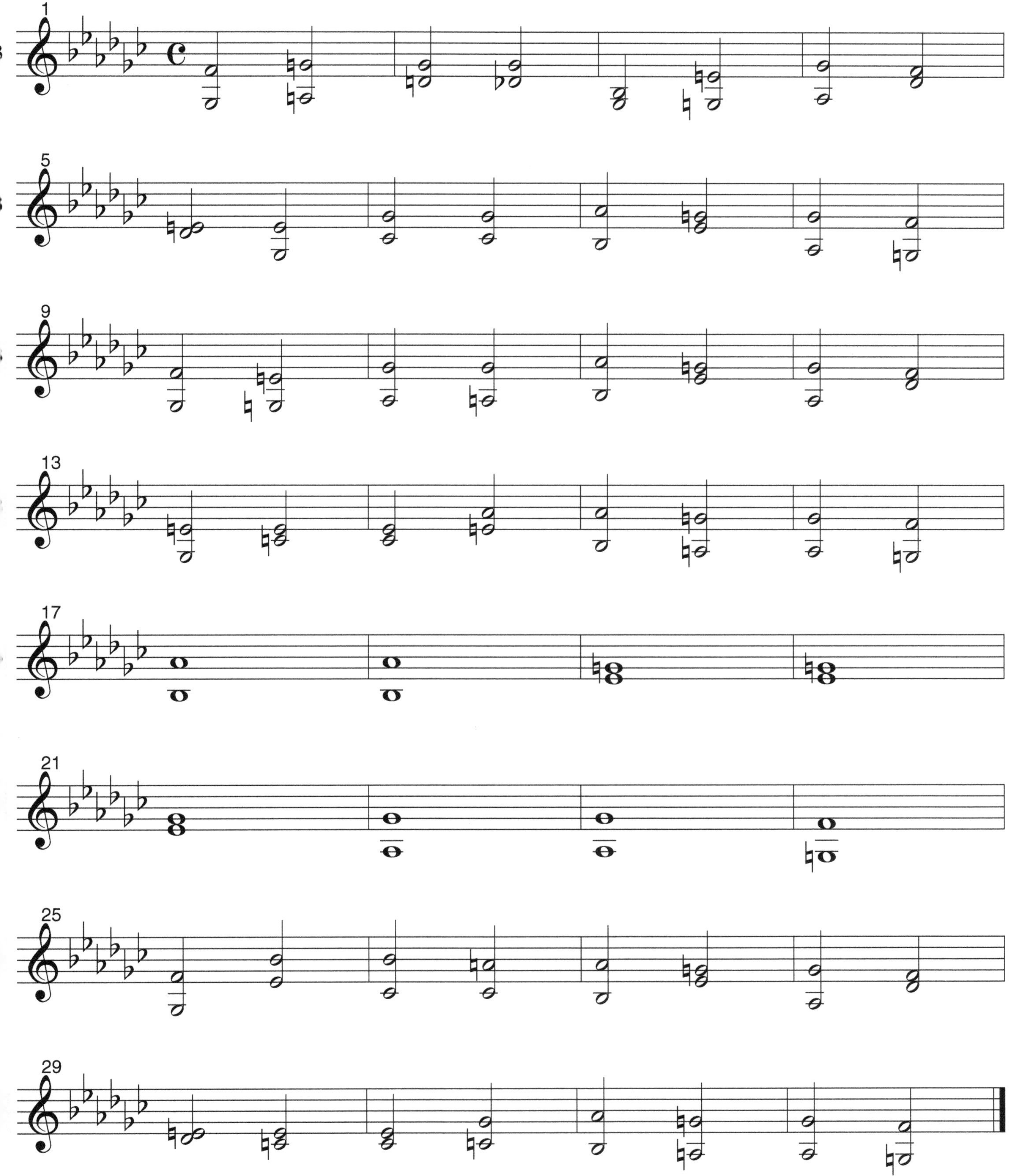

Directions:
Advanced Students
1. Sing top melody using solfeggio while playing bottom part
2. Sing bottom melody using solfeggio while playing top part

Directions for reading for piano or guitar
Advanced Students
1. Sight read both parts as written and 8va

Exercise 66

Directions for singing:
Advanced Students
1. Sing top melody using solfeggio while playing bottom part
2. Sing bottom melody using solfeggio while playing top part

Directions for reading for piano or guitar
Advanced Students
1. Sight read both parts as written and 8va

Exercise 67

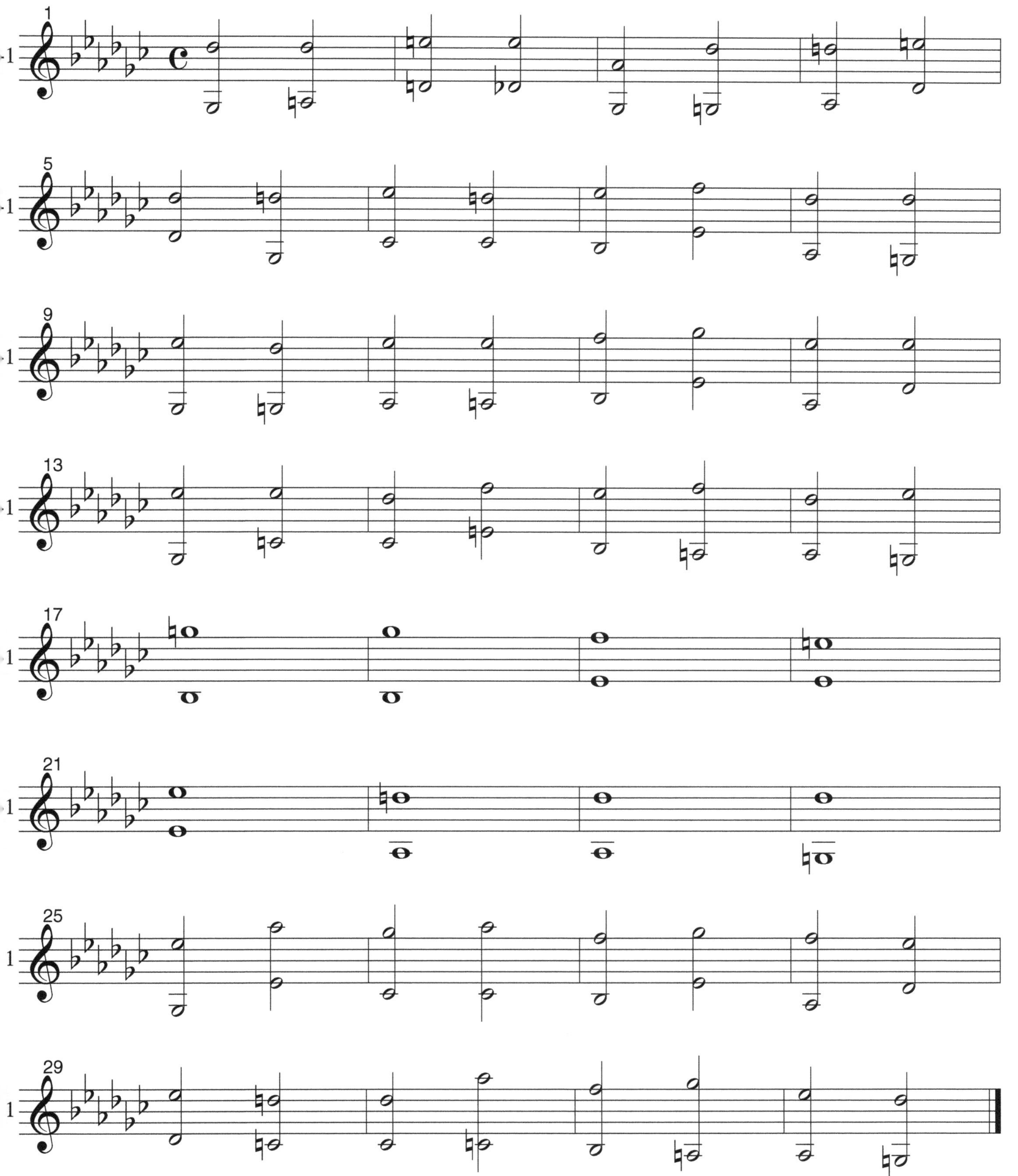

Directions for singing:
Advanced Students
1. Sing top melody using solfeggio while playing bottom part
2. Sing bottom melody using solfeggio while playing top part

Directions for reading for piano or guitar
Advanced Students
1. Sight read both parts as written and 8va

Exercise 68

Directionsfor singing:
Advanced Students
1. Sing top melody using solfeggio while playing bottom two parts
2. Sing middle melody using solfeggio while playing top and bottom parts
2. Sing bottom melody using solfeggio while playing upper two parts

Directions for reading for piano or guit
Advanced Students
1. Sight read all parts as written and 8

Exercise 69

Directions for singing:
Advanced Students
1. Sing top melody using solfeggio while playing bottom two parts
2. Sing middle melody using solfeggio while playing top and bottom parts
2. Sing bottom melody using solfeggio while playing upper two parts

Directions for reading for piano or guitar
Advanced Students
1. Sight read all parts as written and 8va

Exercise 70

Directions:
Advanced Students
1. Sing top melody using solfeggio while playing bottom three parts
2. Sing 2nd voice using solfeggio while playing other voices
3. Sing 3nd voice using solfeggio while playing other voices
4. Sing bottom voice using solfeggio while playing upper three parts

Directions for reading for piano or guitar
Advanced Students
1. Sight read all parts as written and 8va

Exercise 71

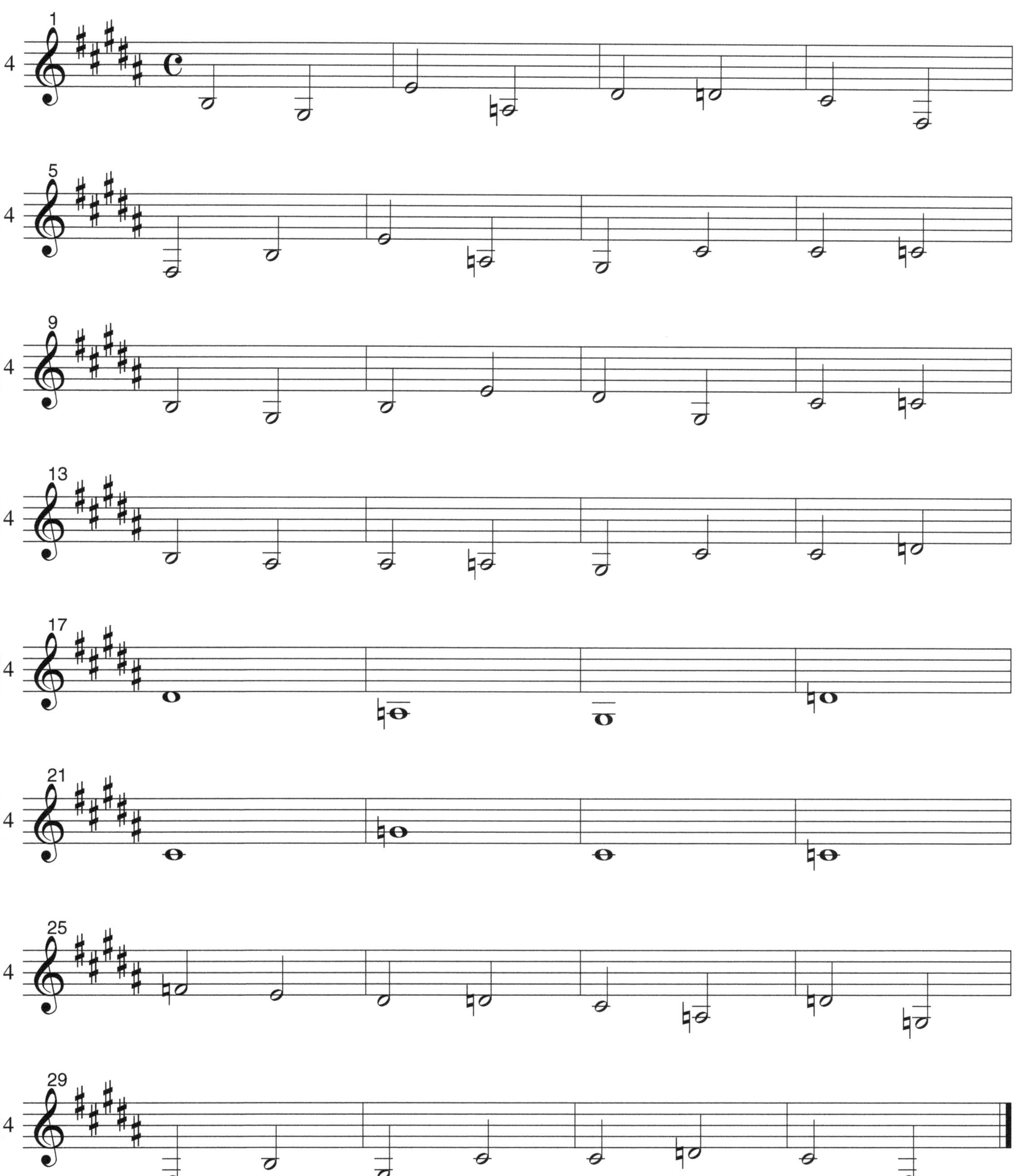

Directions for Singing:
Beginning Student
1. Sing melody using solfeggio while playing a B Major Chord
Advanced Student
1. Sing melody using solfeggio with no accompaniment

Directions for Reading:
All Students
1. Sight read as written and 8va

Exercise 72

Directions for Singing:
Beginning Student
1. Sing melody using solfeggio while playing a B Major Chord
Advanced Student
1. Sing melody using solfeggio with no accompaniment

Directions for Reading:
All Students
1. Sight read as written and 8va

Exercise 73

Directions for Singing:
Beginning Student
1. Sing melody using solfeggio while playing a B Major Chord
Advanced Student
1. Sing melody using solfeggio with no accompaniment

Directions for Reading:
All Students
1. Sight read as written and 8va

Exercise 74

Directions for Singing:
Beginning Student
1. Sing melody using solfeggio while playing a B Major Chord
Advanced Student
1. Sing melody using solfeggio with no accompaniment

Directions for Reading:
All Students
1. Sight read as written and 8va

Exercise 75

Directions:
Advanced Students
1. Sing top melody using solfeggio while playing bottom part
2. Sing bottom melody using solfeggio while playing top part

Directions for reading for piano or guitar
Advanced Students
1. Sight read both parts as written and 8va

Exercise 76

Directions for singing:
Advanced Students
1. Sing top melody using solfeggio while playing bottom part
2. Sing bottom melody using solfeggio while playing top part

Directions for reading for piano or guitar
Advanced Students
1. Sight read both parts as written and 8va

Exercise 77

Directions for singing:
Advanced Students
1. Sing top melody using solfeggio while playing bottom part
2. Sing bottom melody using solfeggio while playing top part

Directions for reading for piano or guitar
Advanced Students
1. Sight read both parts as written and 8va

Exercise 78

Directionsfor singing:
Advanced Students
1. Sing top melody using solfeggio while playing bottom two parts
2. Sing middle melody using solfeggio while playing top and bottom parts
2. Sing bottom melody using solfeggio while playing upper two parts

Directions for reading for piano or guita
Advanced Students
1. Sight read all parts as written and 8va

Exercise 79

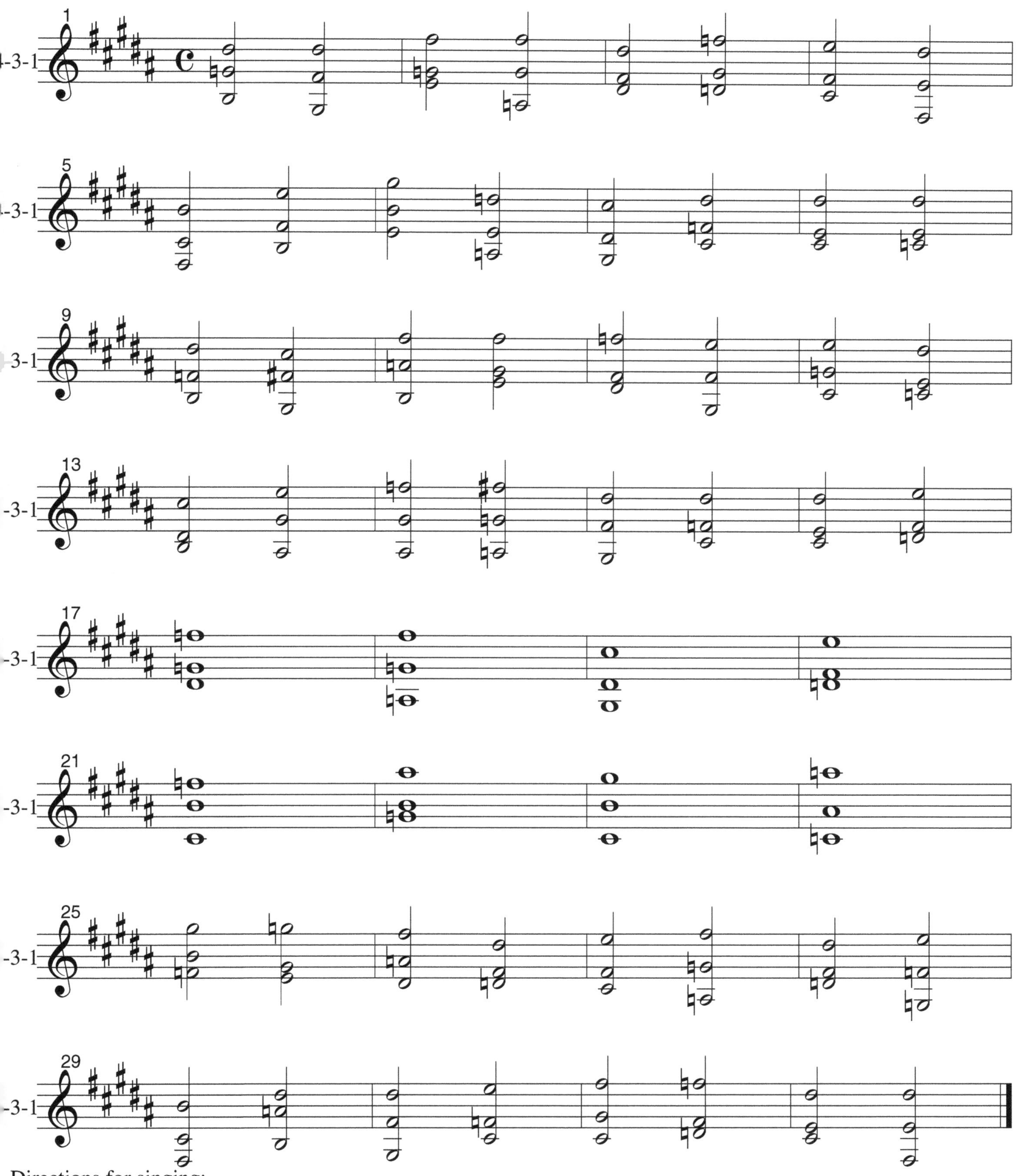

Directions for singing:
Advanced Students
1. Sing top melody using solfeggio while playing bottom two parts
2. Sing middle melody using solfeggio while playing top and bottom parts
2. Sing bottom melody using solfeggio while playing upper two parts

Directions for reading for piano or guitar
Advanced Students
1. Sight read all parts as written and 8va

Exercise 80

Directions:
Advanced Students
1. Sing top melody using solfeggio while playing bottom three parts
2. Sing 2nd voice using solfeggio while playing other voices
3. Sing 3nd voice using solfeggio while playing other voices
4. Sing bottom voice using solfeggio while playing upper three parts

Directions for reading for piano or guitar
Advanced Students
1. Sight read all parts as written and 8va

Exercise 81

Directions for Singing:
Beginning Student
1. Sing melody using solfeggio while playing a E Major Chord
Advanced Student
1. Sing melody using solfeggio with no accompaniment

Directions for Reading:
All Students
1. Sight read as written and 8va

Exercise 82

Directions for Singing:
Beginning Student
1. Sing melody using solfeggio while playing a E Major Chord
Advanced Student
1. Sing melody using solfeggio with no accompaniment

Directions for Reading:
All Students
1. Sight read as written and 8va

Exercise 83

Directions for Singing:
Beginning Student
1. Sing melody using solfeggio while playing a E Major Chord
Advanced Student
1. Sing melody using solfeggio with no accompaniment

Directions for Reading:
All Students
1. Sight read as written and 8va

Exercise 84

Directions for Singing:
Beginning Student
1. Sing melody using solfeggio while playing a E Major Chord
Advanced Student
1. Sing melody using solfeggio with no accompaniment

Directions for Reading:
All Students
1. Sight read as written and 8va

Exercise 85

Directions:
Advanced Students
1. Sing top melody using solfeggio while playing bottom part
2. Sing bottom melody using solfeggio while playing top part

Directions for reading for piano or guitar
Advanced Students
1. Sight read both parts as written and 8va

Exercise 86

Directions for singing:
Advanced Students
1. Sing top melody using solfeggio while playing bottom part
2. Sing bottom melody using solfeggio while playing top part

Directions for reading for piano or guitar
Advanced Students
1. Sight read both parts as written and 8va

Exercise 87

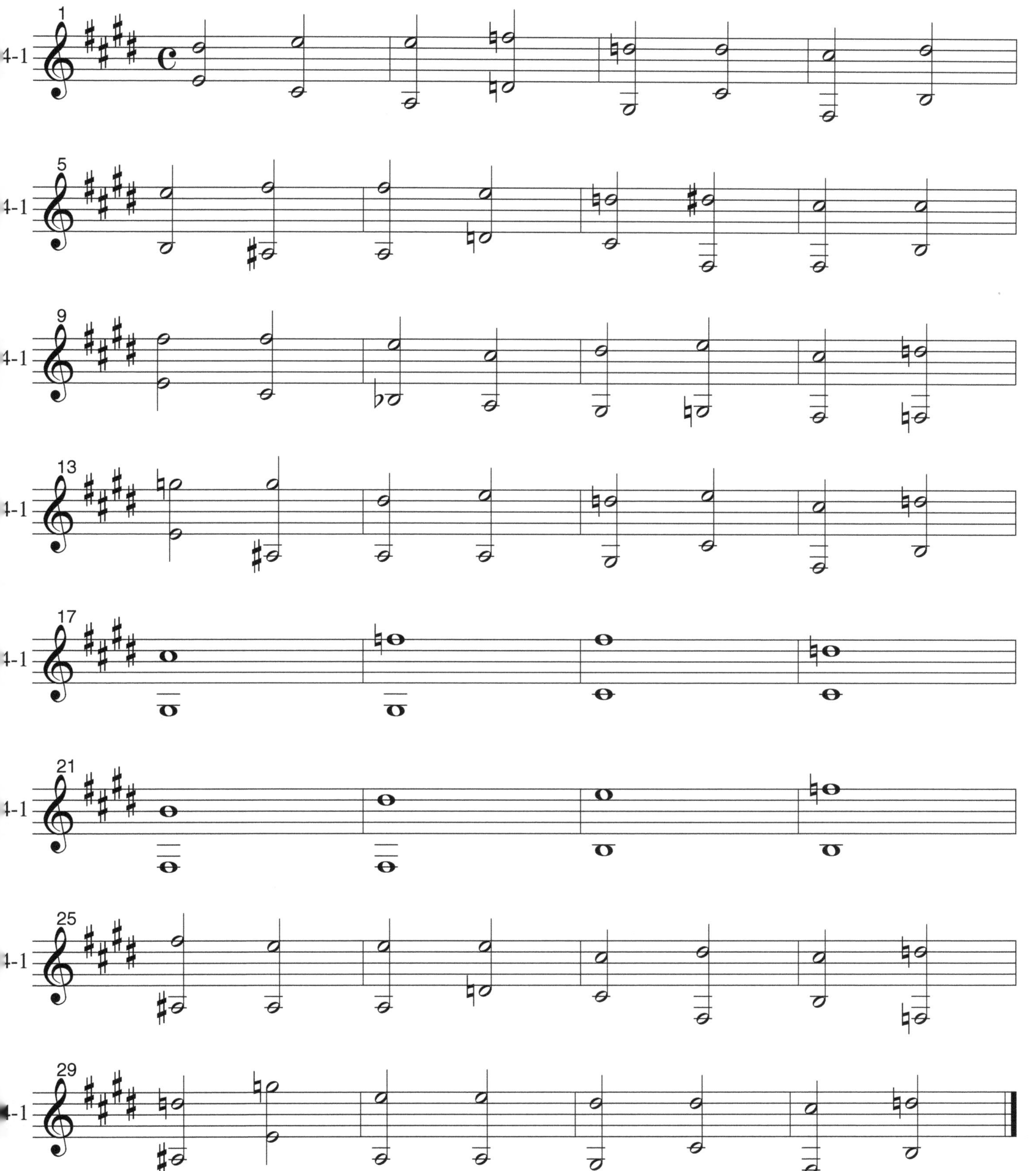

Directions for singing:
Advanced Students
1. Sing top melody using solfeggio while playing bottom part
2. Sing bottom melody using solfeggio while playing top part

Directions for reading for piano or guitar
Advanced Students
1. Sight read both parts as written and 8va

Exercise 88

Directionsfor singing:
Advanced Students
1. Sing top melody using solfeggio while playing bottom two parts
2. Sing middle melody using solfeggio while playing top and bottom parts
2. Sing bottom melody using solfeggio while playing upper two parts

Directions for reading for piano or guit
Advanced Students
1. Sight read all parts as written and 8v

Exercise 89

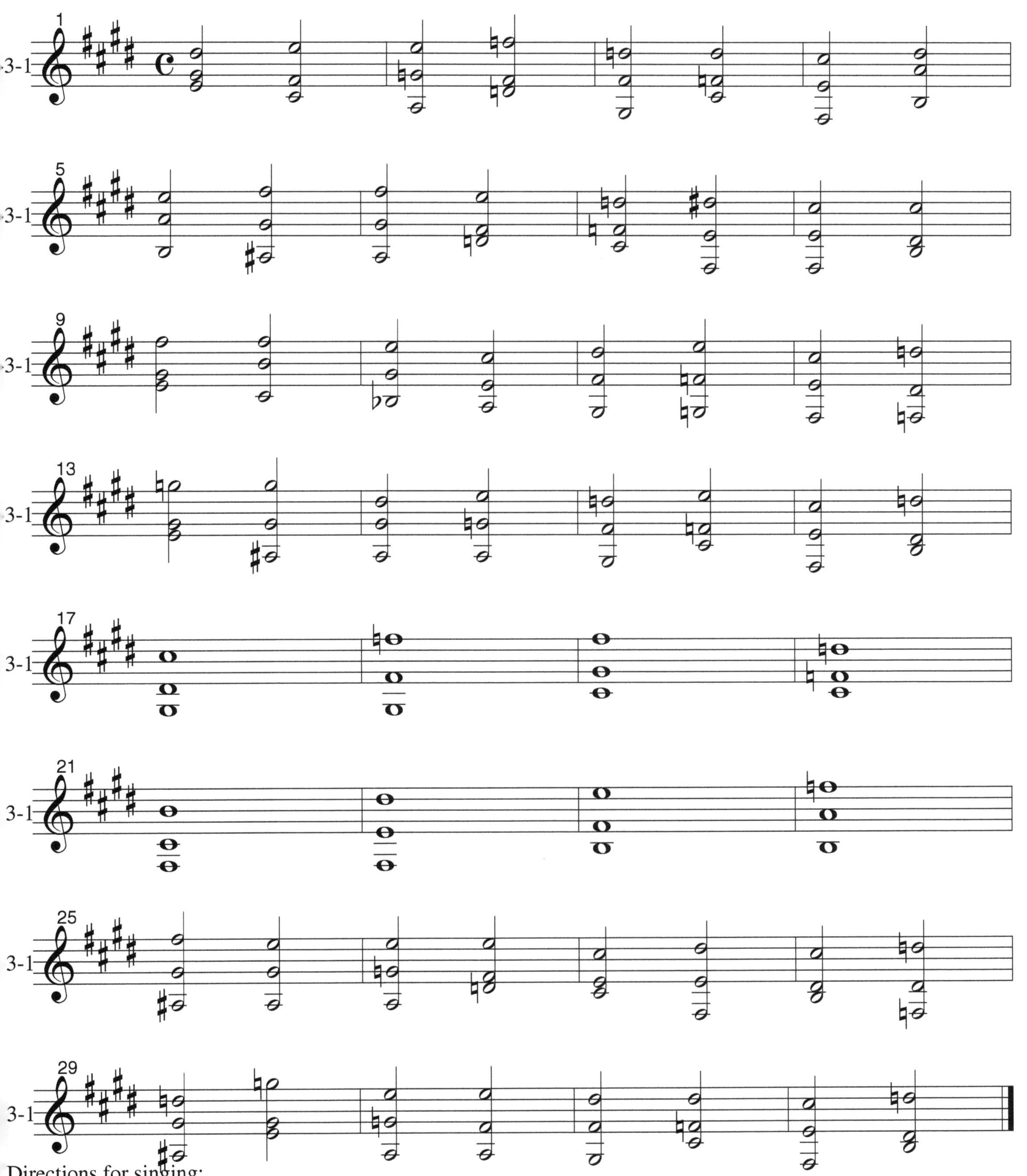

Directions for singing:
Advanced Students
1. Sing top melody using solfeggio while playing bottom two parts
2. Sing middle melody using solfeggio while playing top and bottom parts
2. Sing bottom melody using solfeggio while playing upper two parts

Directions for reading for piano or guitar
Advanced Students
1. Sight read all parts as written and 8va

Exercise 90

Directions:
Advanced Students
1. Sing top melody using solfeggio while playing bottom three parts
2. Sing 2nd voice using solfeggio while playing other voices
3. Sing 3nd voice using solfeggio while playing other voices
4. Sing bottom voice using solfeggio while playing upper three parts

Directions for reading for piano or guitar
Advanced Students
1. Sight read all parts as written and 8va

Exercise 91

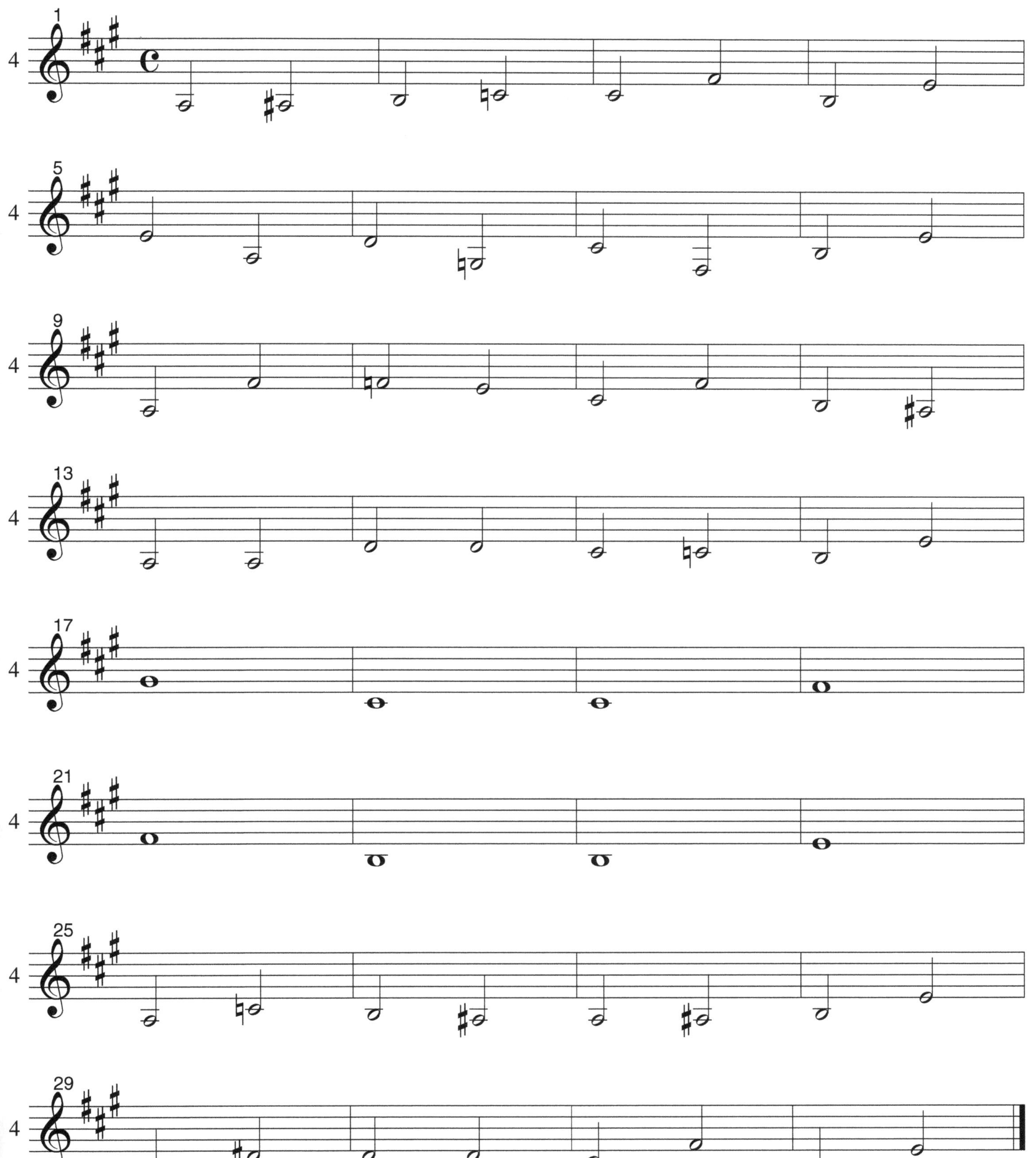

Directions for Singing:
Beginning Student
1. Sing melody using solfeggio while playing a A Major Chord
Advanced Student
1. Sing melody using solfeggio with no accompaniment

Directions for Reading:
All Students
1. Sight read as written and 8va

Exercise 92

Directions for Singing:
Beginning Student
1. Sing melody using solfeggio while playing a A Major Chord
Advanced Student
1. Sing melody using solfeggio with no accompaniment

Directions for Reading:
All Students
1. Sight read as written and 8va

Exercise 93

Directions for Singing:
Beginning Student
1. Sing melody using solfeggio while playing a A Major Chord
Advanced Student
1. Sing melody using solfeggio with no accompaniment

Directions for Reading:
All Students
1. Sight read as written and 8va

Exercise 94

Directions for Singing:
Beginning Student
1. Sing melody using solfeggio while playing a A Major Chord
Advanced Student
1. Sing melody using solfeggio with no accompaniment

Directions for Reading:
All Students
1. Sight read as written and 8va

Exercise 95

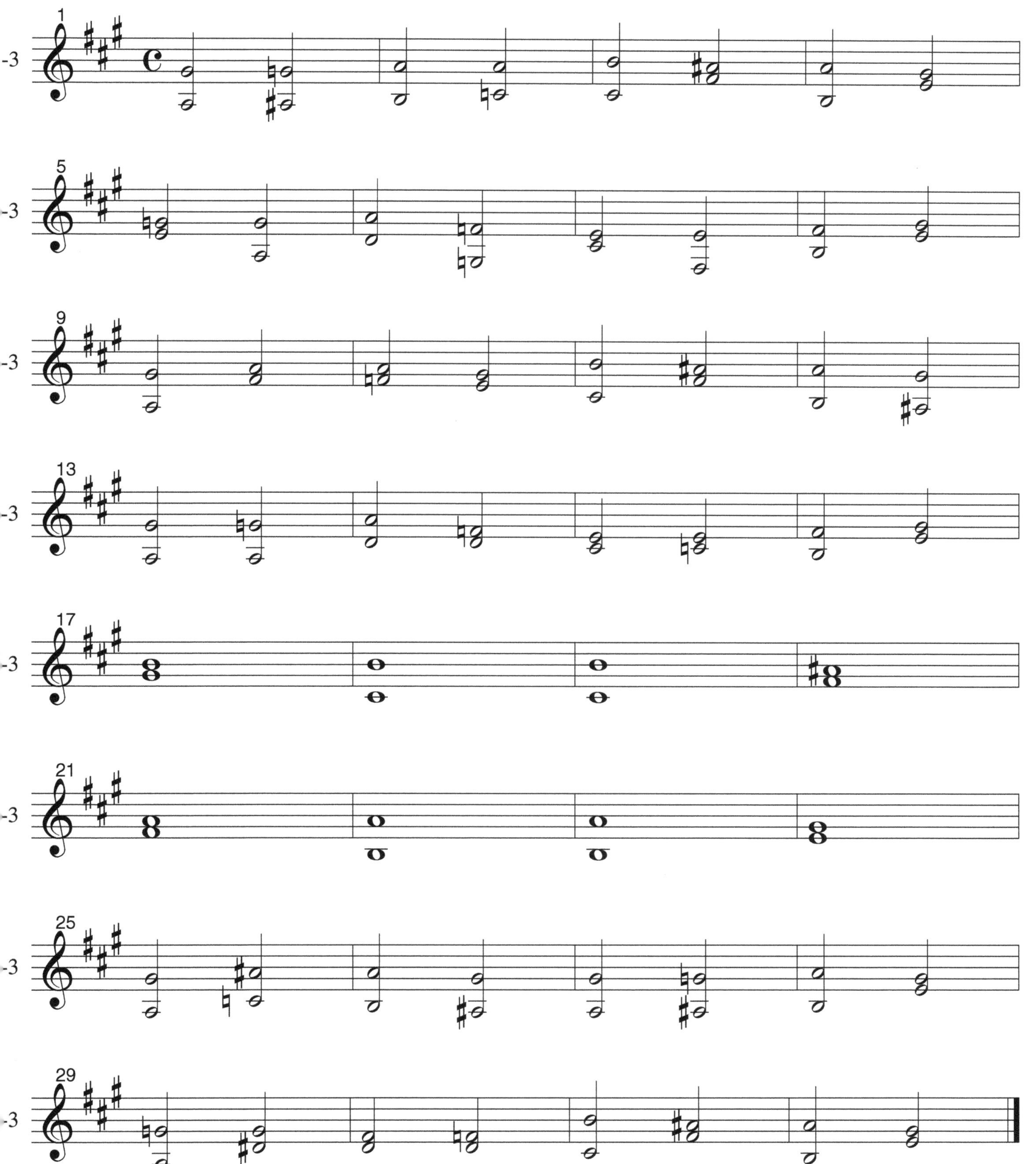

Directions:
Advanced Students
1. Sing top melody using solfeggio while playing bottom part
2. Sing bottom melody using solfeggio while playing top part

Directions for reading for piano or guitar
Advanced Students
1. Sight read both parts as written and 8va

Exercise 96

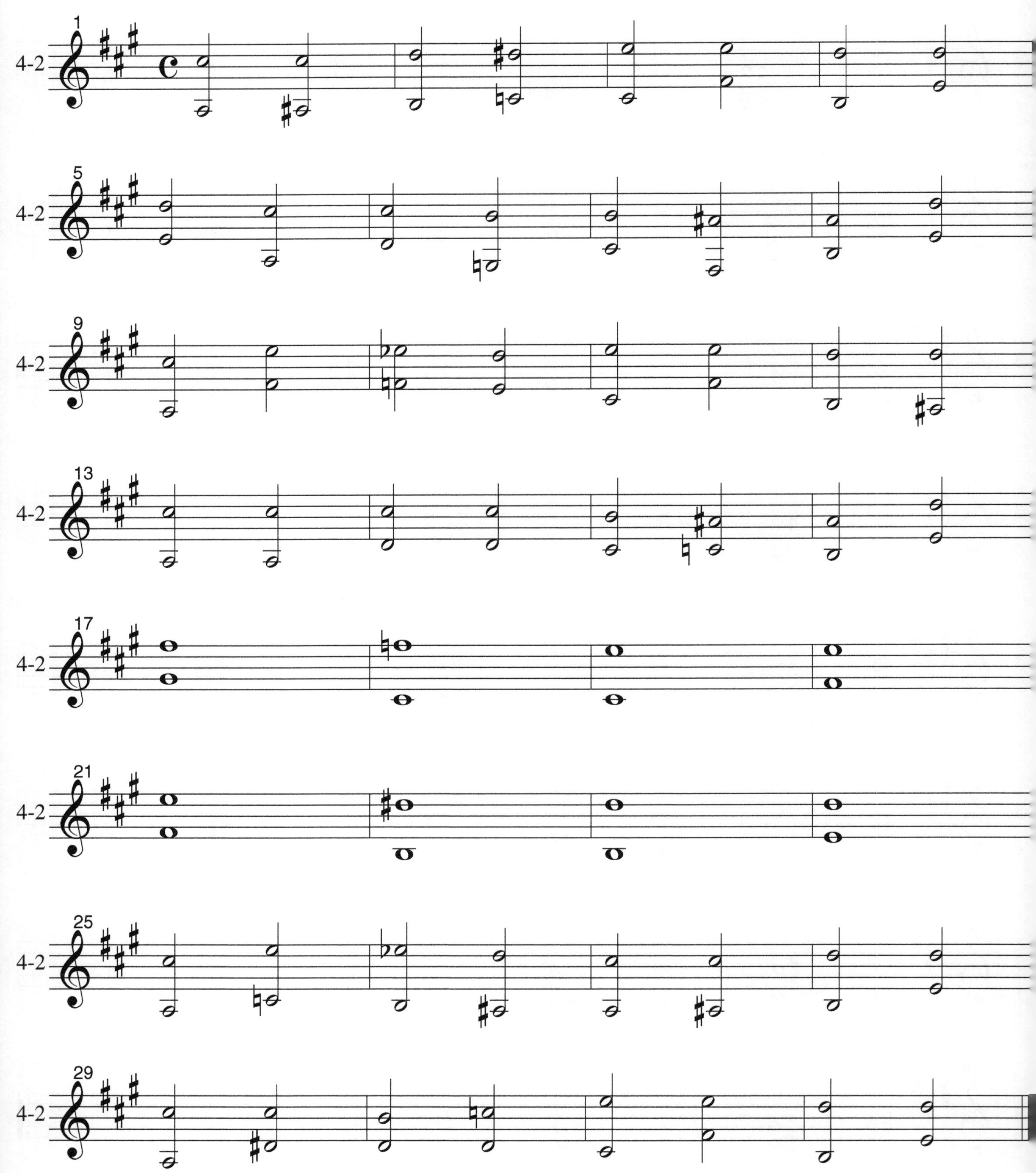

Directions for singing:
Advanced Students
1. Sing top melody using solfeggio while playing bottom part
2. Sing bottom melody using solfeggio while playing top part

Directions for reading for piano or guitar
Advanced Students
1. Sight read both parts as written and 8v.

Exercise 97

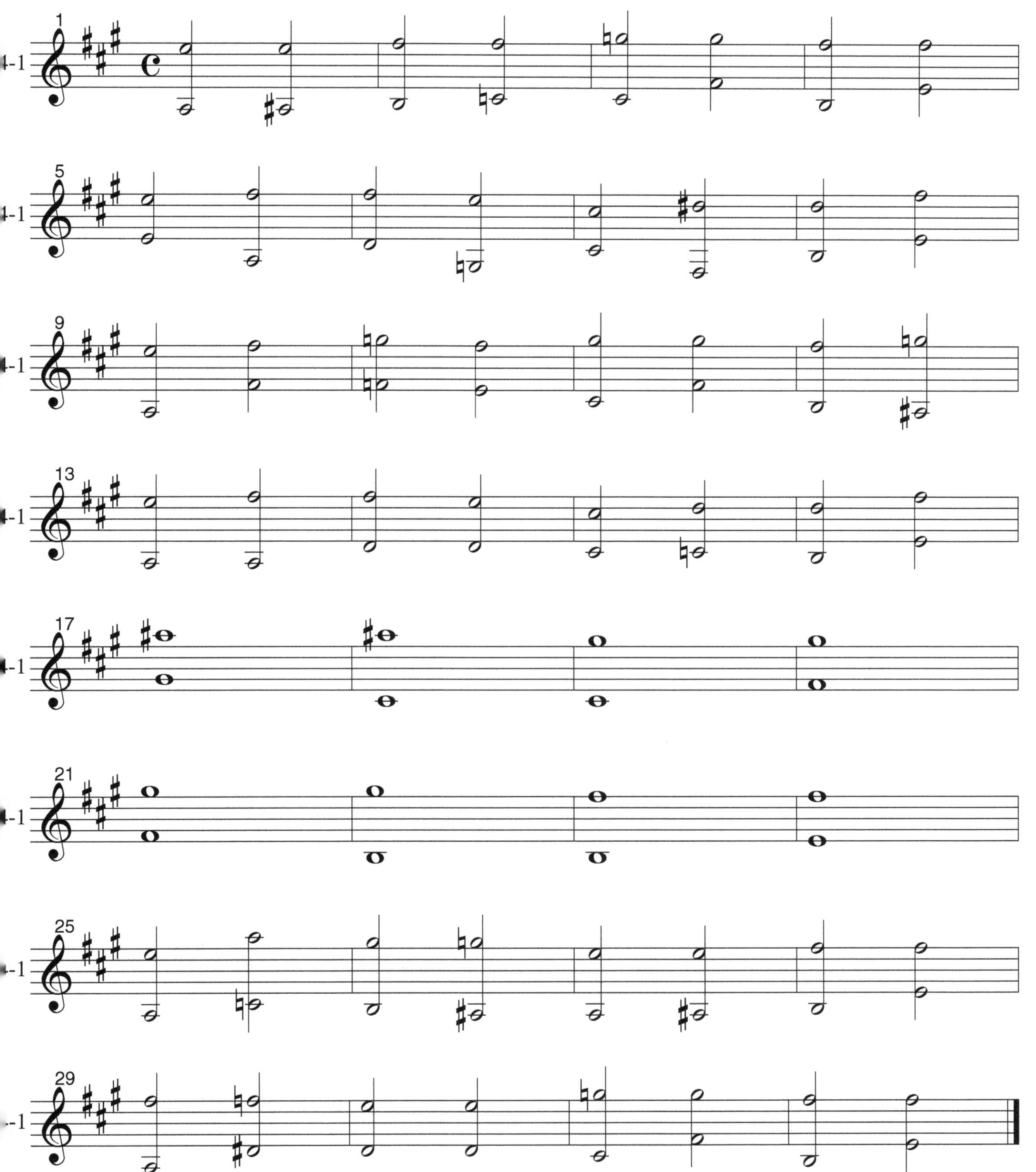

Directions for singing:
Advanced Students
1. Sing top melody using solfeggio while playing bottom part
2. Sing bottom melody using solfeggio while playing top part

Directions for reading for piano or guitar
Advanced Students
1. Sight read both parts as written and 8va

Exercise 98

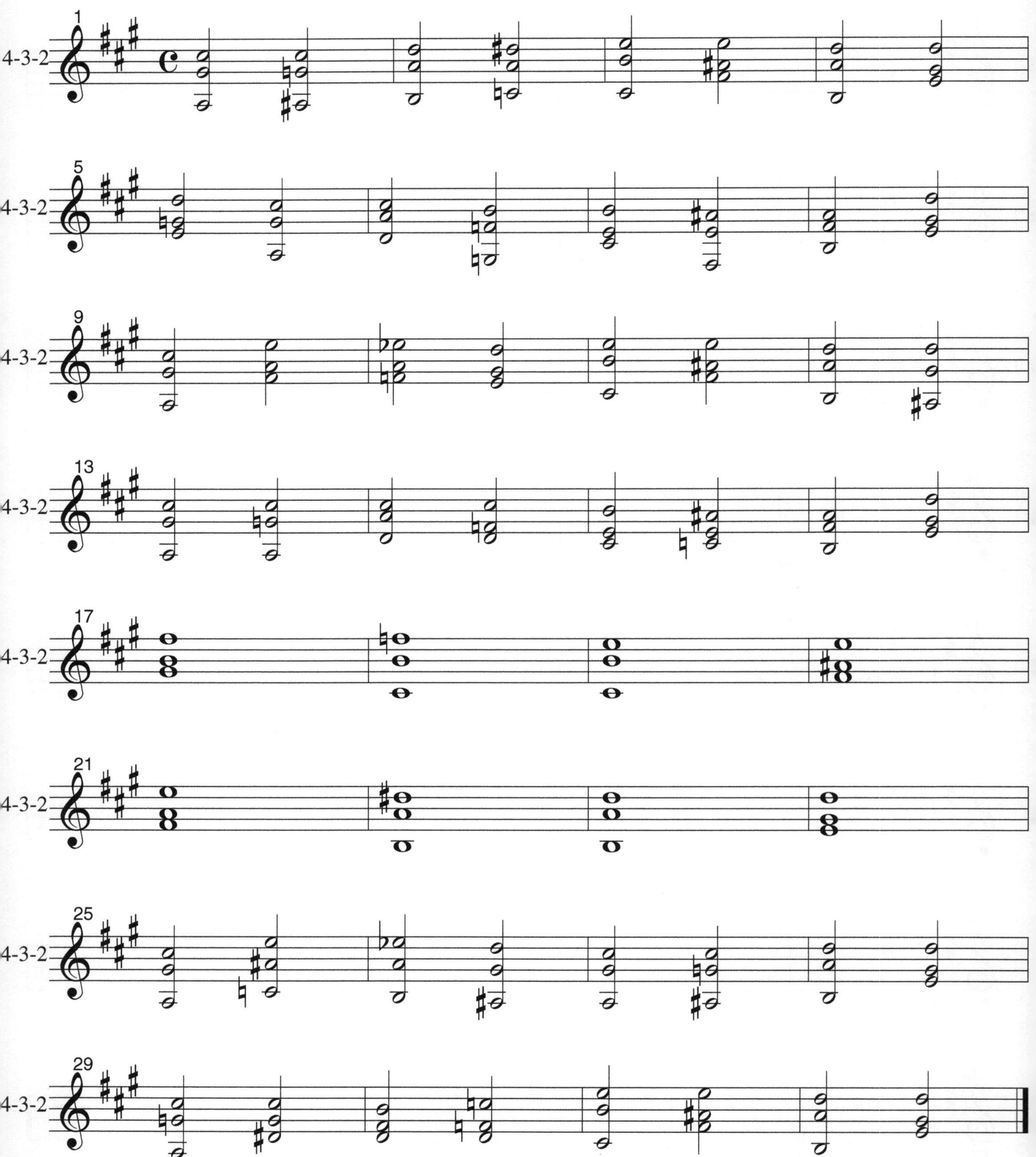

Directionsfor singing:
Advanced Students
1. Sing top melody using solfeggio while playing bottom two parts
2. Sing middle melody using solfeggio while playing top and bottom parts
2. Sing bottom melody using solfeggio while playing upper two parts

Directions for reading for piano or guita
Advanced Students
1. Sight read all parts as written and 8v.

Exercise 99

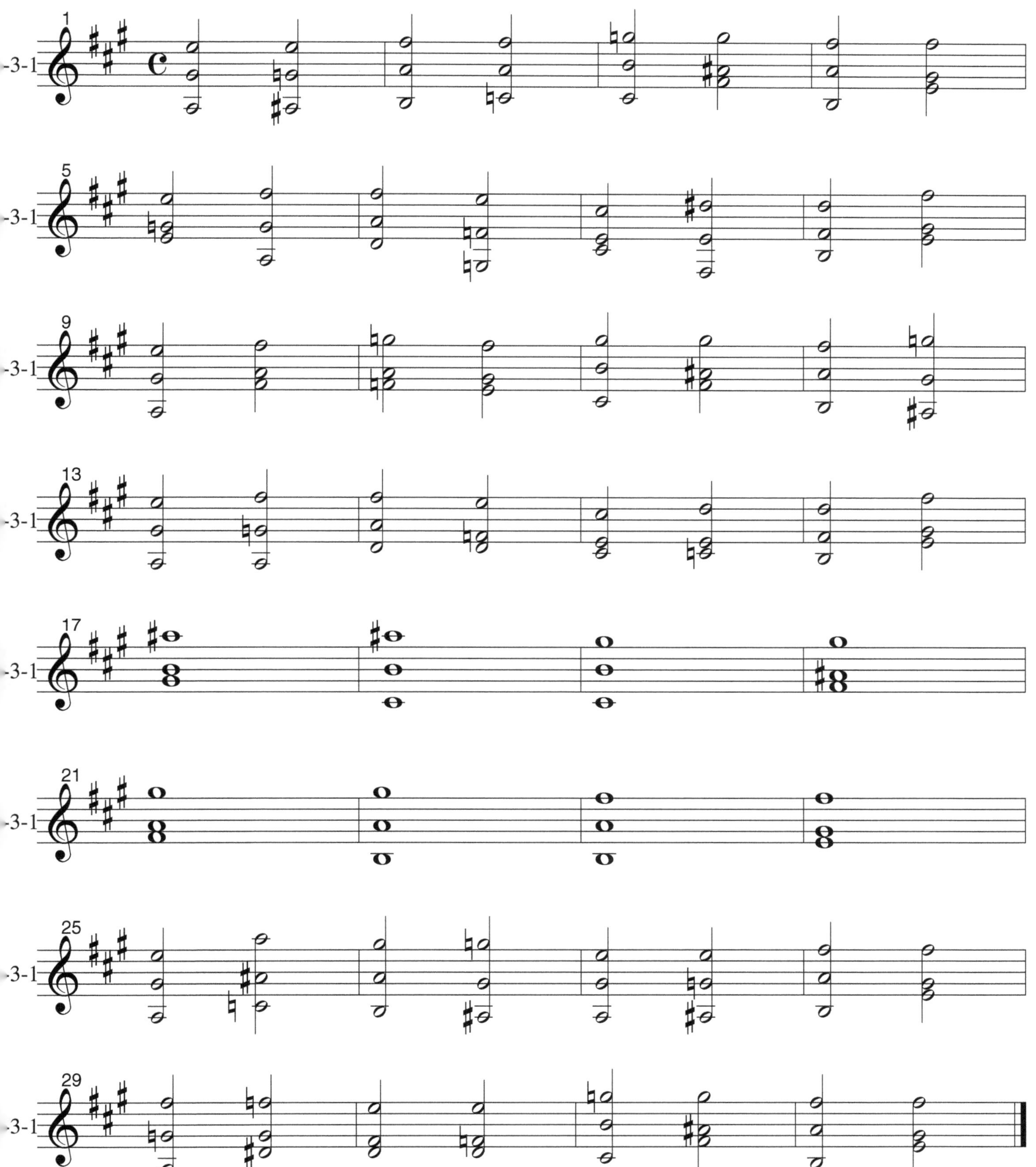

Directions for singing:
Advanced Students
1. Sing top melody using solfeggio while playing bottom two parts
2. Sing middle melody using solfeggio while playing top and bottom parts
2. Sing bottom melody using solfeggio while playing upper two parts

Directions for reading for piano or guitar
Advanced Students
1. Sight read all parts as written and 8va

Exercise 100

Directions:
Advanced Students
1. Sing top melody using solfeggio while playing bottom three parts
2. Sing 2nd voice using solfeggio while playing other voices
3. Sing 3nd voice using solfeggio while playing other voices
4. Sing bottom voice using solfeggio while playing upper three parts

Directions for reading for piano or guitar
Advanced Students
1. Sight read all parts as written and 8va

Exercise 101

Directions for Singing:
Beginning Student
1. Sing melody using solfeggio while playing a D Major Chord
Advanced Student
1. Sing melody using solfeggio with no accompaniment

Directions for Reading:
All Students
1. Sight read as written and 8va

Exercise 102

Directions for Singing:
Beginning Student
1. Sing melody using solfeggio while playing a D Major Chord
Advanced Student
1. Sing melody using solfeggio with no accompaniment

Directions for Reading:
All Students
1. Sight read as written and 8va

Exercise 103

Directions for Singing:
Beginning Student
1. Sing melody using solfeggio while playing a D Major Chord
Advanced Student
1. Sing melody using solfeggio with no accompaniment

Directions for Reading:
All Students
1. Sight read as written and 8va

Exercise 104

Directions for Singing:
Beginning Student
1. Sing melody using solfeggio while playing a D Major Chord
Advanced Student
1. Sing melody using solfeggio with no accompaniment

Directions for Reading:
All Students
1. Sight read as written and 8va

Exercise 105

Directions:
Advanced Students
1. Sing top melody using solfeggio while playing bottom part
2. Sing bottom melody using solfeggio while playing top part

Directions for reading for piano or guitar
Advanced Students
1. Sight read both parts as written and 8va

Exercise 106

Directions for singing:
Advanced Students
1. Sing top melody using solfeggio while playing bottom part
2. Sing bottom melody using solfeggio while playing top part

Directions for reading for piano or guitar
Advanced Students
1. Sight read both parts as written and 8v

Exercise 107

Directions for singing:
Advanced Students
1. Sing top melody using solfeggio while playing bottom part
2. Sing bottom melody using solfeggio while playing top part

Directions for reading for piano or guitar
Advanced Students
1. Sight read both parts as written and 8va

Exercise 108

Directionsfor singing:
Advanced Students
1. Sing top melody using solfeggio while playing bottom two parts
2. Sing middle melody using solfeggio while playing top and bottom parts
2. Sing bottom melody using solfeggio while playing upper two parts

Directions for reading for piano or guit
Advanced Students
1. Sight read all parts as written and 8v

Exercise 109

Directions for singing:
Advanced Students
1. Sing top melody using solfeggio while playing bottom two parts
2. Sing middle melody using solfeggio while playing top and bottom parts
2. Sing bottom melody using solfeggio while playing upper two parts

Directions for reading for piano or guitar
Advanced Students
1. Sight read all parts as written and 8va

Exercise 110

Directions:
Advanced Students
1. Sing top melody using solfeggio while playing bottom three parts
2. Sing 2nd voice using solfeggio while playing other voices
3. Sing 3nd voice using solfeggio while playing other voices
4. Sing bottom voice using solfeggio while playing upper three parts

Directions for reading for piano or guitar
Advanced Students
1. Sight read all parts as written and 8va

Exercise 111

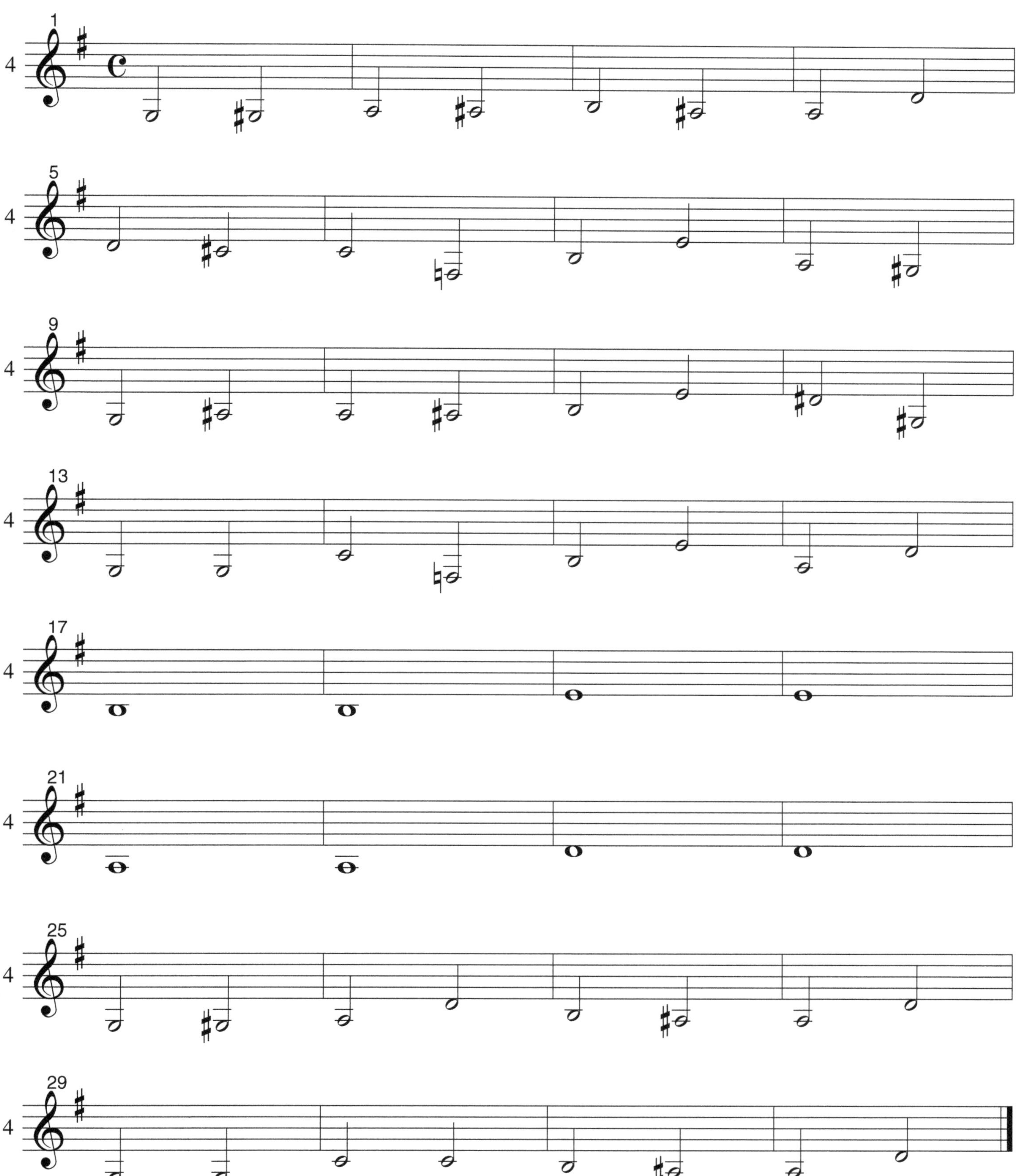

Directions for Singing:
Beginning Student
1. Sing melody using solfeggio while playing a G Major Chord
Advanced Student
1. Sing melody using solfeggio with no accompaniment

Directions for Reading:
All Students
1. Sight read as written and 8va

Exercise 112

Directions for Singing:
Beginning Student
1. Sing melody using solfeggio while playing a G Major Chord
Advanced Student
1. Sing melody using solfeggio with no accompaniment

Directions for Reading:
All Students
1. Sight read as written and 8va

Exercise 113

Directions for Singing:
Beginning Student
1. Sing melody using solfeggio while playing a G Major Chord
Advanced Student
1. Sing melody using solfeggio with no accompaniment

Directions for Reading:
All Students
1. Sight read as written and 8va

Exercise 114

Directions for Singing:
Beginning Student
1. Sing melody using solfeggio while playing a G Major Chord
Advanced Student
1. Sing melody using solfeggio with no accompaniment

Directions for Reading:
All Students
1. Sight read as written and 8va

Exercise 115

Directions:
Advanced Students
1. Sing top melody using solfeggio while playing bottom part
2. Sing bottom melody using solfeggio while playing top part

Directions for reading for piano or guitar
Advanced Students
1. Sight read both parts as written and 8va

Exercise 116

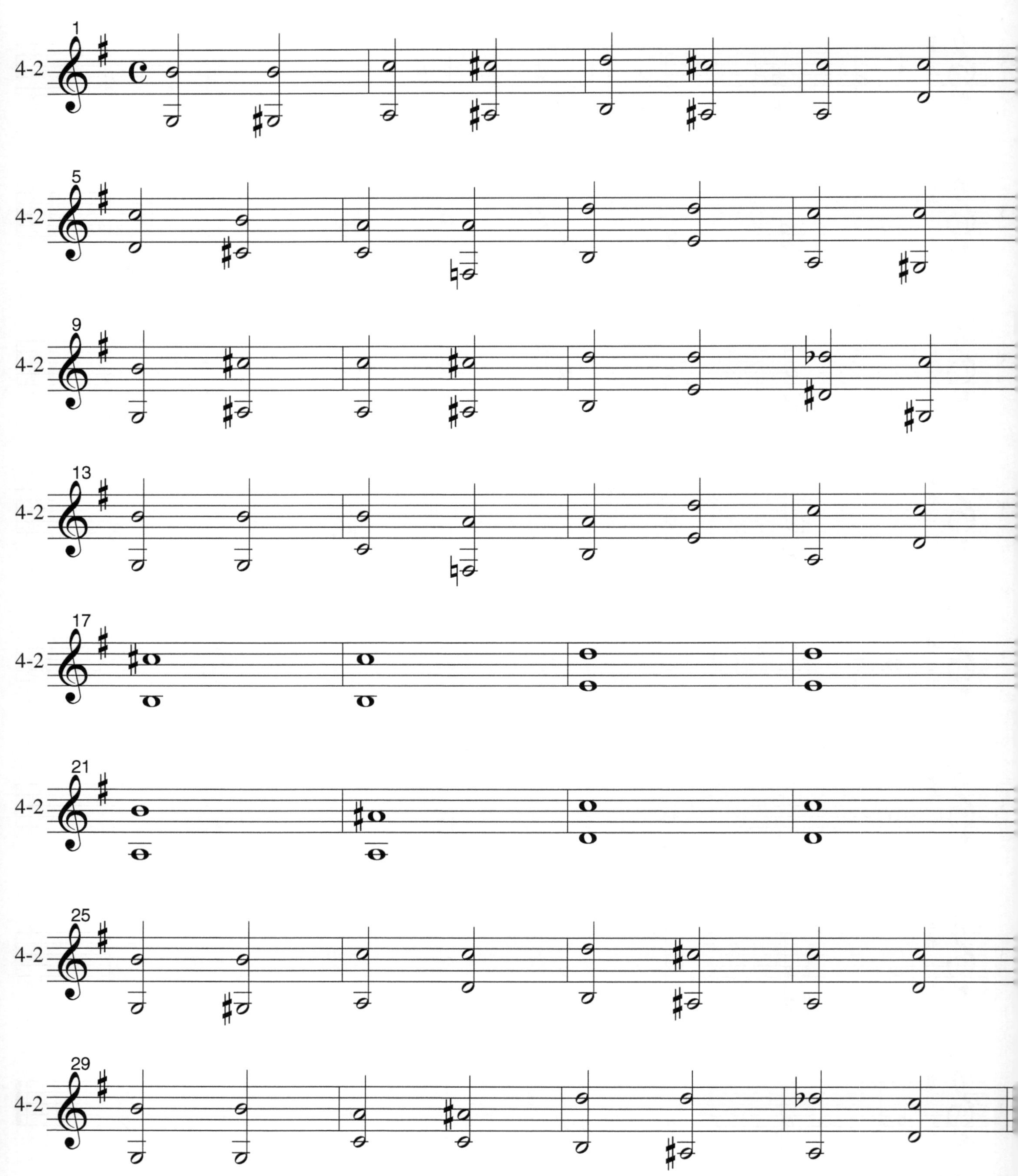

Directions for singing:
Advanced Students
1. Sing top melody using solfeggio while playing bottom part
2. Sing bottom melody using solfeggio while playing top part

Directions for reading for piano or guitar
Advanced Students
1. Sight read both parts as written and 8va

Exercise 117

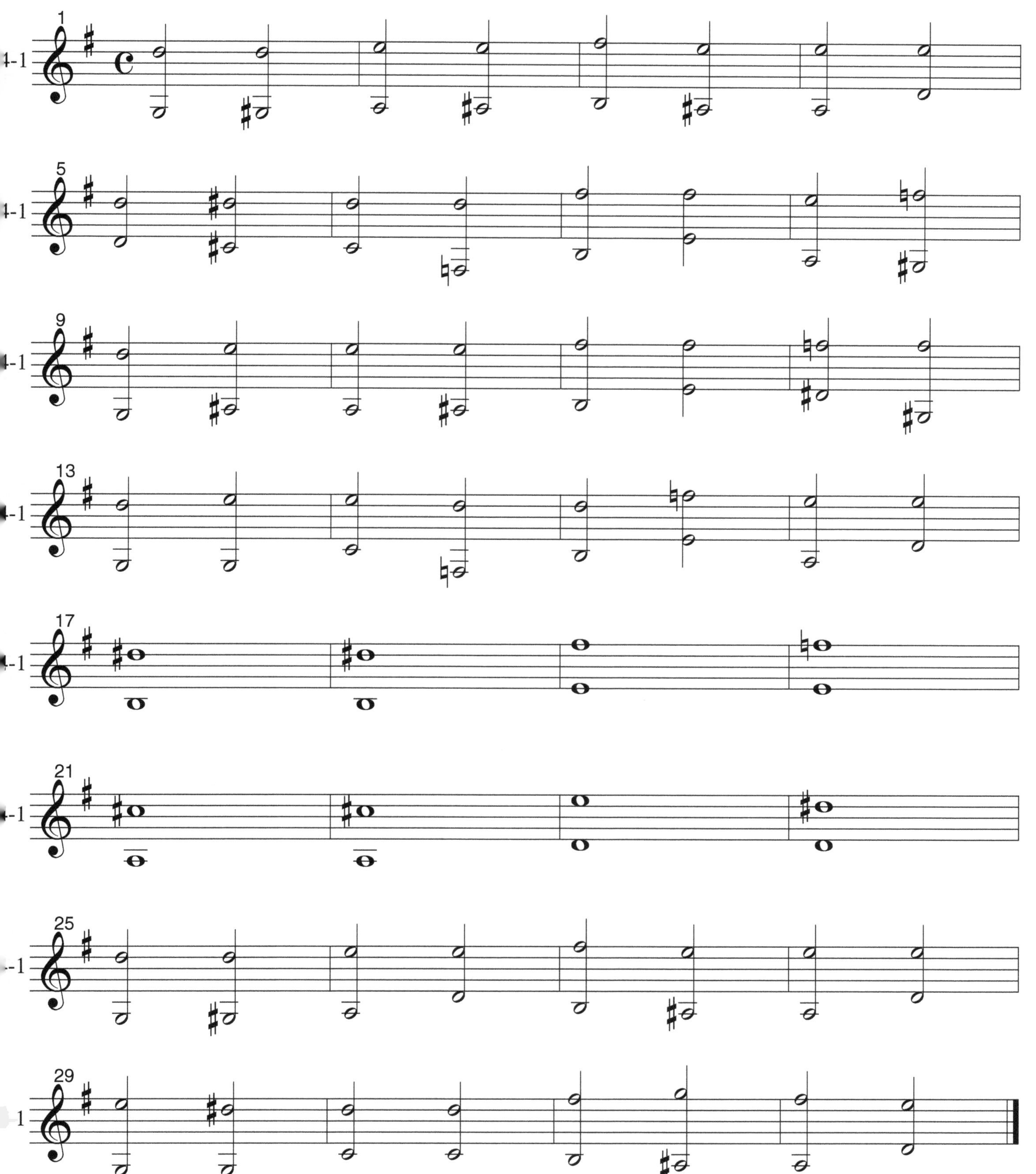

Directions for singing:
Advanced Students
1. Sing top melody using solfeggio while playing bottom part
2. Sing bottom melody using solfeggio while playing top part

Directions for reading for piano or guitar
Advanced Students
1. Sight read both parts as written and 8va

Exercise 118

Directions for singing:
Advanced Students
1. Sing top melody using solfeggio while playing bottom two parts
2. Sing middle melody using solfeggio while playing top and bottom parts
2. Sing bottom melody using solfeggio while playing upper two parts

Directions for reading for piano or guit
Advanced Students
1. Sight read all parts as written and 8v

Exercise 119

Directions for singing:
Advanced Students
1. Sing top melody using solfeggio while playing bottom two parts
2. Sing middle melody using solfeggio while playing top and bottom parts
2. Sing bottom melody using solfeggio while playing upper two parts

Directions for reading for piano or guitar
Advanced Students
1. Sight read all parts as written and 8va

Exercise 120

Directions:
Advanced Students
1. Sing top melody using solfeggio while playing bottom three parts
2. Sing 2nd voice using solfeggio while playing other voices
3. Sing 3nd voice using solfeggio while playing other voices
4. Sing bottom voice using solfeggio while playing upper three parts

Directions for reading for piano or guitar
Advanced Students
1. Sight read all parts as written and 8va

Books Available From
Muse Eek Publishing Company

The Bruce Arnold series of instruction books for guitar are the result of 20 years of teaching. Mr. Arnold, who teaches at New York University and Princeton University has listened to the questions and problems of his students, and written forty books addressing the needs of the beginning to advanced student. Written in a direct, friendly and practical manner, each book is structured in such as way as to enable a student to understand, retain and apply musical information. In short, these books teach.

1st Steps for a Beginning Guitarist
Spiral Bound ISBN 1890944-90-4 Perfect Bound ISBN 1890944-93-9

"1st Steps for a Beginning Guitarist" is a comprehensive method for guitar students who have no prior musical training. Whether you are playing acoustic, electric or twelve-string guitar, this book will give you the information you need, and trouble shoot the various pitfalls that can hinder the self-taught musician. Includes pictures, videos and audio in the form of midifiles and mp3's.

Chord Workbook for Guitar Volume 1 (2nd edition)
Spiral Bound ISBN 0-9648632-1-9 Perfect Bound ISBN 1890944-50-5

A consistent seller, this book addresses the needs of the beginning through intermediate student. The beginning student will learn chords on the guitar, and a section is also included to help learn the basics of music theory. Progressions are provided to help the student apply these chords to common sequences. The more advanced student will find the reharmonization section to be an invaluable resource of harmonic choices. Information is given through musical notation as well as tablature.

Chord Workbook for Guitar Volume 2 (2nd edition)
Spiral Bound ISBN 0-9648632-3-5 Perfect Bound ISBN 1890944-51-3

This book is the Rosetta Stone of pop/jazz chords, and is geared to the intermediate to advanced student. These are the chords that any serious student bent on a musical career must know. Unlike other books which simply give examples of isolated chords, this unique book provides a comprehensive series of progressions and chord combinations which are immediately applicable to both composition and performance.

Music Theory Workbook for Guitar Series

The world's most popular instrument, the guitar, is not taught in our public schools. In addition, it is one of the hardest on which to learn the basics of music. As a result, it is frequently difficult for the serious guitarist to get a firm foundation in theory.

Theory Workbook for Guitar Volume 1
Spiral Bound ISBN 0-9648632-4-3 Perfect Bound ISBN 1890944-52-1

This book provides real hands-on application of intervals and chords. A theory section written in concise and easy to understand language prepares the student for all exercises. Worksheets are given that quiz a student about intervals and chord construction using staff notation and guitar tablature. Answers are supplied in the back of the book enabling a student to work without a teacher.

Theory Workbook for Guitar Volume 2
Spiral Bound ISBN 0-9648632-5-1 Perfect Bound ISBN 1890944-53-X

This book provides real hands-on application for 22 different scale types. A theory section written in concise and easy to understand language prepares the student for all exercises. Worksheets are given that quiz a student about scale construction using staff notation and guitar tablature. Answers are supplied in the back of the book enabling a student to work without a teacher. Audio files are also available on the muse-eek.com website to facilitate practice and improvisation with all the scales presented.

Rhythm Book Series

These books are a breakthrough in music instruction, using the internet as a teaching tool! Audio files of all the exercises are easily downloaded from the internet.

Rhythm Primer
Spiral Bound ISBN 0-890944-03-3 Perfect Bound ISBN 1890944-59-9

This 61 page book concentrates on all basic rhythms using four rhythmic levels. All examples use one pitch, allowing the student to focus completely on time and rhythm. All exercises can be downloaded from the internet to facilitate learning. See http://www.muse-eek.com for details

Rhythms Volume 1
Spiral Bound ISBN 0-9648632-7-8 Perfect Bound ISBN 1890944-55-6

This 120 page book concentrates on eighth note rhythms and is a thesaurus of rhythmic patterns. All examples use one pitch, allowing the student to focus completely on time and rhythm. All exercises can be downloaded from the internet to facilitate learning. See http://www.muse-eek.com for details.

Rhythms Volume 2
Spiral Bound ISBN 0-9648632-8-6 Perfect Bound ISBN 1890944-56-4

This volume concentrates on sixteenth note rhythms, and is a 108 page thesaurus of rhythmic patterns. All examples use one pitch, allowing the student to focus completely on time and rhythm. All exercises can be downloaded from the internet to facilitate learning. See http://www.muse-eek.com for details.

Rhythms Volume 3
Spiral Bound ISBN 0-890944-04-1 Perfect Bound ISBN 1890944-57-2

This volume concentrates on thirty second note rhythms, and is a 102 page thesaurus of rhythmic patterns. All examples use one pitch, allowing the student to focus completely on time and rhythm. All exercises can be downloaded from the internet to facilitate learning. See http://www.muse-eek.com for details.

Odd Meters Volume 1
Spiral Bound ISBN 0-9648632-9-4 Perfect Bound ISBN 1890944-58-0

This book applies both eighth and sixteenth note rhythms to odd meter combinations. All examples use one pitch, allowing the student to focus completely on time and rhythm. Exercises can be downloaded from the internet to facilitate learning. This 100 page book is an essential sight reading tool.
See http://www.muse-eek.com for details.

Contemporary Rhythms Volume 1

Spiral Bound ISBN 1-890944-27-0 Perfect Bound ISBN 1890944-84-X

This volume concentrates on eight note rhythms and is a thesaurus of rhythmic patterns. Each exercise uses one pitch which allows the student to focus completely on time and rhythm. Exercises use modern innovations common to twentieth century notation, thereby familiarizing the student with the most sophisticated systems likely to be encountered in the course of a musical career. All exercises can be downloaded from the internet to facilitate learning. See http://www.muse-eek.com for details.

Contemporary Rhythms Volume 2

Spiral Bound ISBN 1-890944-28-9 Perfect Bound ISBN 1890944-85-8

This volume concentrates on sixteenth note rhythms and is a thesaurus of rhythmic patterns. Each exercise uses one pitch which allows the student to focus completely on time and rhythm. Exercise use modern innovations common to twentieth century notation, thereby familiarizing the student with the most sophisticated systems likely to be encountered in the course of a musical career. All exercises can be downloaded from the internet to facilitate learning. See http://www.muse-eek.com for details.

Independence Volume 1

Spiral Bound ISBN 1-890944-00-9 Perfect Bound ISBN 1890944-83-1

This 51 page book is designed for pianists, stick and touchstyle guitarists, percussionists and anyone who wishes to develop the rhythmic independence of their hands. This volume concentrates on quarter, eighth and sixteenth note rhythms and is a thesaurus of rhythmic patterns. The exercises in this book gradually incorporate more and more complex rhythmic patterns making it an excellent tool for both the beginning and the advanced student.

Other Guitar Study Aids

Right Hand Technique for Guitar Volume 1

Spiral Bound ISBN 0-9648632-6-X Perfect Bound ISBN 1890944-54-8

Here's a breakthrough in music instruction, using the internet as a teaching tool! This book gives a concise method for developing right hand technique on the guitar, one of the most overlooked and under-addressed aspects of learning the instrument. The simplest, most basic movements are used to build fatigue-free technique. Exercises can be downloaded from the internet to facilitate learning. See http://www.muse-eek.com for details.

Single String Studies Volume One

Spiral Bound ISBN 1-890944-01-7 Perfect Bound ISBN 1890944-62-9

This book is an excellent learning tool for both the beginner who has no experience reading music on the guitar, and the advanced student looking to improve their ledger line reading and general knowledge of each string of the guitar. Each exercise concentrates the students attention on one string at a time. This allows a familiarity to form between the written pitch and where it can be found on the guitar along with improving one's "feel" for jumping linearly across the fretboard. Exercises can be downloaded from the internet to facilitate learning. See http://www.muse-eek.com for details.

Single String Studies Volume Two
Spiral Bound ISBN 1-890944-05-X   Perfect Bound ISBN 1890944-64-5

This book is a continuation of Volume One, but using non-diatonic notes. Volume Two helps the intermediate and advanced student improve their ledger line reading and general knowledge of each string of the guitar. Each exercise concentrates the students attention on one string at a time. This allows a familiarity to form between the written pitch and where it can be found on the guitar along with improving one's "feel" for jumping linearly across the fretboard. Exercises can be downloaded from the internet to facilitate learning. See http://www.muse-eek.com for details.

Single String Studies Volume One (Bass Clef)
Spiral Bound ISBN 1-890944-02-5   Perfect Bound ISBN 1890944-63-7

This book is an excellent learning tool for both the beginner who has no experience reading music on the bass guitar, and the advanced student looking to improve their ledger line reading and general knowledge of each string of the bass. Each exercise concentrates a students attention of one string at a time. This allows a familiarity to form between the written pitch and where it can be found on the bass along with improving one's "feel" for jumping linearly across the fretboard. Exercises can be downloaded from the internet to facilitate learning. See http://www.muse-eek.com for details.

Single String Studies Volume Two (Bass Clef)
Spiral Bound ISBN 1-890944-06-8   Perfect Bound ISBN 1890944-65-3

This book is a continuation of Volume One, but using non-diatonic notes. Volume Two helps the intermediate and advanced student improve their ledger line reading and general knowledge of each string of the bass. Each exercise concentrates the students attention on one string at a time. This allows a familiarity to form between the written pitch and where it can be found on the bass along with improving one's "feel" for jumping linearly across the fretboard. Exercises can be downloaded from the internet to facilitate learning. See http://www.muse-eek.com for details.

Guitar Clinic
Spiral Bound ISBN 1-890944-45-9   Perfect Bound ISBN 1890944-86-6

Guitar Clinic" contains techniques and exercises Mr. Arnold uses in the clinics and workshops he teaches around the U.S.. Much of the material in this book is culled from Mr. Arnold's educational series, over thirty books in all. The student wishing to expand on his or her studies will find suggestions within the text as to which of Mr. Arnold's books will best serve their specific needs. Topics covered include: how to read music, sight reading, reading rhythms, music theory, chord and scale construction, modal sequencing, approach notes, reharmonization, bass and chord comping, and hexatonic scales.

Sight Singing and Ear Training Series

<u>The world is full of ear training and sight reading books, so why do we need more?</u> *This sight singing and ear training series uses a different method of teaching relative pitch sight singing and ear training. The success of this method has been remarkable. Along with a new method of ear training these books also use CDs and the internet as a teaching tool! Audio files of all the exercises are easily downloaded from the internet at www.muse-eek.com By combining interactive audio files with a new approach to ear training a student's progress is limited only by their willingness to practice!*

A Fanatic's Guide to Ear Training and Sight Singing

Spiral Bound ISBN 1-890944-19-X   Perfect Bound ISBN 1890944-75-0

This book and CD present a method for developing good pitch recognition through sight singing. This method differs from the myriad of other sight singing books in that it develops the ability to identify and name all twelve pitches within a key center. Through this method a student gains the ability to identify sound based on it's relationship to a key and not the relationship of one note to another (i.e. interval training as commonly taught in many texts). All note groupings from one to six notes are presented giving the student a thesaurus of basic note combinations which develops sight singing and note recognition to a level unattainable before this Guide's existence.

Key Note Recognition

Spiral Bound ISBN 1-890944-30-0   Perfect Bound ISBN 1890944-77-7

This book and CD present a method for developing the ability to recognize the function of any note against a key. This method is a must for anyone who wishes to sound one note on an instrument or voice and instantly know what key a song is in. Through this method a student gains the ability to identify a sound based on its relationship to a key and not the relationship of one note to another (i.e. interval training as commonly taught in many texts). Key Center Recognition is a definite requirement before proceeding to two note ear training.

LINES Volume One: Sight Reading and Sight Singing Exercises

Spiral Bound ISBN 1-890944-09-2   Perfect Bound ISBN 1890944-76-9

This book can be used for many applications. It is an excellent source for easy half note melodies that a beginner can use to learn how to read music or for sight singing slightly chromatic lines. An intermediate or advanced student will find exercises for multi-voice reading. These exercises can also be used for multi-voice ear training. The book has the added benefit in that all exercises can be heard by downloading the audio files for each example. See http://www.muse-eek.com for details.

Ear Training ONE NOTE: Beginning Level

Spiral Bound ISBN 1-890944-12-2   Perfect Bound ISBN 1890944-66-1

This is a new method for developing instantaneous recognition of pitches within a key. This contextual-based ear training differs from interval based training by instilling a sense of key relationship; that is, a note is identified by it's characteristic sound within a key, and not by its distance from another note. This method has been used with great success and is now finally available on CD. There are three levels available depending on the student's ability. This beginning level is recommended for students who have little or no music training. A Complete Method book containing the Ear Training One Note Beginning, Intermediate and Advanced levels along with three accompanying CDs is also available for those students wishing to have a complete set of books and CDs under one cover.

Ear Training ONE NOTE: Intermediate Level
Spiral Bound ISBN 1-890944-13-0   Perfect Bound ISBN 1890944-67-X

This is a new method for developing instantaneous recognition of pitches within a key. This contextual-based ear training differs from interval based training by instilling a sense of key relationship; that is, a note is identified by it's characteristic sound within a key, and not by its distance from another note. This method has been used with great success and is now finally available on CD. There are three levels available depending on the student's ability. This intermediate level is recommended for students who have had some music training but still find their skills need more development. A Complete Method book containing the Ear Training One Note Beginning, Intermediate and Advanced levels along with three accompanying CDs is also available for those students wishing to have a complete set of books and CDs under one cover.

Ear Training ONE NOTE: Advanced Level
Spiral Bound ISBN 1-890944-14-9   Perfect Bound ISBN 1890944-68-8

This is a new method for developing instantaneous recognition of pitches within a key. This contextual-based ear training differs from interval based training by instilling a sense of key relationship; that is, a note is identified by it's characteristic sound within a key, and not by its distance from another note. This method has been used with great success and is now finally available on CD. There are three levels available depending on the student's ability. This advanced level is recommended for advanced music students or those who have worked with the intermediate level and now wish to perfect their skills. A Complete Method book containing the Ear Training One Note Beginning, Intermediate and Advanced levels along with three accompanying CDs is also available for those students wishing to have a complete set of books and CDs under one cover.

Ear Training ONE NOTE: Complete Method
Spiral Bound ISBN 1-890944-47-5   Perfect Bound ISBN 1890944-48-3

This is a new method for developing instantaneous recognition of pitches within a key. This contextual-based ear training differs from interval based training by instilling a sense of key relationship; that is, a note is identified by it's characteristic sound within a key, and not by its distance from another note. This Complete Method book contains the Ear Training One Note Beginning, Intermediate and Advanced levels along with three accompanying CDsand is available for those students who wish to have a complete set of books and CDs under one cover.

Ear Training TWO NOTE: Beginning Level Volume One
Spiral Bound ISBN 1-890944-31-9   Perfect Bound ISBN 1890944-69-6

This Book and Audio CD continues the method of developing relative pitch ear training as set forth in the "Ear Training, One Note" series. There are six volumes in the beginning level series. Through practice, the student eventually gains the ability to recognize the key and the names of any two notes played simultaneously. Volume One concentrates on 5ths. Prerequisite: a strong grasp of the One Note method.

Ear Training TWO NOTE: Beginning LevelVolume Two
Spiral Bound ISBN 1-890944-32-7 Perfect Bound ISBN 1890944-70-X

This Book and Audio CD continues the method of developing relative pitch ear training as set forth in the "Ear Training, One Note" series. There are six volumes in the beginning level series. Through practice, the student eventually gains the ability to recognize the key and the names of any two notes played simultaneously. Volume Two concentrates on 3rds. Prerequisite: a strong grasp of the One Note method.

Ear Training TWO NOTE: Beginning Level Volume Three
Spiral Bound ISBN 1-890944-33-5 Perfect Bound ISBN 1890944-71-8

This Book and Audio CD continues the method of developing relative pitch ear training as set forth in the "Ear Training, One Note" series. There are six volumes in the beginning level series. Through practice, the student eventually gains the ability to recognize the key and the names of any two notes played simultaneously. Volume Three concentrates on 6ths. Prerequisite: a strong grasp of the One Note method.

Ear Training TWO NOTE: Beginning Level Volume Four
Spiral Bound ISBN 1-890944-34-3 Perfect Bound ISBN 1890944-72-6

This Book and Audio CD continues the method of developing relative pitch ear training as set forth in the "Ear Training, One Note" series. There are six volumes in the beginning level series. Through practice, the student eventually gains the ability to recognize the key and the names of any two notes played simultaneously. Volume Four concentrates on 4ths. Prerequisite: a strong grasp of the One Note method.

Ear Training TWO NOTE: Beginning Level Volume Five
Spiral Bound ISBN 1-890944-35-1 Perfect Bound ISBN 1890944-73-4

This Book and Audio CD continues the method of developing relative pitch ear training as set forth in the "Ear Training, One Note" series. There are six volumes in the beginning level series. Through practice, the student eventually gains the ability to recognize the key and the names of any two notes played simultaneously. Volume Five concentrates on 2nds. Prerequisite: a strong grasp of the One Note method.

Ear Training TWO NOTE: Beginning Level Volume Six
Spiral Bound ISBN 1-890944-36-X Perfect Bound ISBN 1890944-74-2

This Book and Audio CD continues the method of developing relative pitch ear training as set forth in the "Ear Training, One Note" series. There are six volumes in the beginning level series. Through practice, the student eventually gains the ability to recognize the key and the names of any two notes played simultaneously. Volume Six concentrates on 7ths. Prerequisite: a strong grasp of the One Note method.

Comping Styles Series

This series is built on the progressions found in Chord Workbook Volume One. Each book covers a specific style of music and presents exercises to help a guitarist, bassist or drummer master that style. Audio CDs are also available so a student can play along with each example and really get "into the groove."

Comping Styles for the Guitar Volume Two FUNK

Spiral Bound ISBN 1-890944-07-6   Perfect Bound ISBN 1890944-60-2

This volume teaches a student how to play guitar or piano in a funk style. 36 Progressions are presented: 12 keys of a Major and Minor Blues plus 12 keys of Rhythm Changes A different groove is presented for each exercise giving the student a wide range of funk rhythms to master. An Audio CD is also included so a student can play along with each example and really get "into the groove." The audio CD contains "trio" versions of each exercise with Guitar, Bass and Drums.

Comping Styles for the Bass Volume Two FUNK

Spiral Bound ISBN 1-890944-08-4   Perfect Bound ISBN 1890944-61-0

This volume teaches a student how to play bass in a funk style. 36 Progressions are presented: 12 keys of a Major and Minor Blues plus 12 keys of Rhythm Changes A different groove is presented for each exercise giving the student a wide range of funk rhythms to master. An Audio CD is also included so a student can play along with each example and really get "into the groove." The audio CD contains "trio" versions of each exercise with Guitar, Bass and Drums.

Bass Lines: Learning and Understanding the Jazz-Blues Bass Line

Spiral Bound ISBN 1-890944-94-7   Perfect Bound ISBN 1890944-95-5

This book covers the basics of bass line construction. A theoretical guide to building bass lines is presented along with 36 chord progressions utilizing the twelve keys of a Major and Minor Blues, plus twelve keys of Rhythm Changes. A reharmonization section is also provided which demonstrates how to reharmonize a chord progression on the spot.

Time Series

The Doing Time series presents a method for contacting, developing and relying on your internal time sense: This series is an excellent source for any musician who is serious about developing strong internal sense of time. This is particularly useful in any kind of music where the rhythms and time signatures may be very complex or free, and there is no conductor.

THE BIG METRONOME

Spiral Bound ISBN 1-890944-37-8   Perfect Bound ISBN 1890944-82-3

The Big Metronome is designed to help you develop a better internal sense of time. This is accomplished by requiring you to "feel time" rather than having you rely on the steady click of a metronome. The idea is to slowly wean yourself away from an external device and rely on your internal/natural sense of time. The exercises presented work in conjunction with the three CDs that accompany this book. CD 1 presents the first 13 settings from a traditional metronome 40-66; the second CD contains metronome markings 69-116, and the third CD contains metronome markings 120-208. The first CD gives you a 2 bar count off and a click every measure, the second CD gives you a 2 bar count off and a click every 2 measures, the 3rd CD gives you a 2 bar count off and a click every 4 measures. By presenting all common metronome markings a student can use these 3 CDs as a replacement for a traditional metronome.

Doing Time with the Blues Volume One:

Spiral Bound ISBN 1-890944-17-3   Perfect Bound ISBN 1890944-78-5

The book and CD presents a method for gaining an internal sense of time thereby eliminating dependence on a metronome. The book presents the basic concept for developing good time and also includes exercises that can be practiced with the CD. The CD provides eight 8 minute tracks at different tempos in which the time is delineated every 2 bars, and with an extra hit every 12 bars to outline the blues form. The student may then use the exercises presented in the book to gain control of their execution or improvise to gain control of their ideas using this bare minimum of time delineation.

Doing Time with the Blues Volume Two:

Spiral Bound ISBN 1-890944-18-1   Perfect Bound ISBN 1890944-79-3

This is the 2nd volume of a four volume series which presents a method for developing a musician's internal sense of time, thereby eliminating dependence on a metronome. This 2nd volume presents different exercises which further the development of this time sense. This 2nd volume begins to test even a professional level player's ability. The CD provides eight 8 minute tracks at different tempos in which the time is delineated every 4 bars with an extra hit every 12 bars to outline the blues form. New exercises are also included that can be practiced with the CD. This series is an excellent source for any musician who is serious about developing an internal sense of time.

Doing Time with 32 bars Volume One:
Spiral Bound ISBN 1-890944-22-X   Perfect Bound ISBN 1890944-80-7

The book and CD presents a method for gaining an internal sense of time thereby eliminating dependence on a metronome. The book presents the basic concept for developing good time and also includes exercises that can be practiced with the CD. The CD provides eight 8 minute tracks at different tempos in which the time is delineated every 2 bars, with an extra hit every 32 to outline the 32 bar form. The student may then use the exercises presented in the book to gain control of their execution or improvise to gain control of their ideas using this bare minimum of time delineation.

Doing Time with 32 bars Volume Two:
Spiral Bound ISBN 1-890944-23-8   Perfect Bound ISBN 1890944-81-5

This is the 2nd volume of a four volume series which presents a method for developing a musician's internal sense of time, thereby eliminating dependence on a metronome.. This 2nd volume presents different exercises which further the development of this time sense. This 2nd volume begins to test even a professional level player's ability. The CD provides eight 8 minute tracks at different tempos in which the time is delineated every 4 bars with an extra hit every 32 bars to outline the 32 bar form. New exercises are also included that can be practiced with the CD. This series is an excellent source for any musician who is serious about developing an internal sense of time.

Other Workbooks

Music Theory Workbook for All Instruments, Volume 1: Interval and Chord Construction
Spiral Bound ISBN 1890944-92-0   Perfect Bound ISBN 1890944-46-7

This book provides real hands-on application of intervals and chords. A theory section written in concise and easy to understand language prepares the student for all exercises. Worksheets are given that quiz a student about intervals and chord construction using staff notation. Answers are supplied in the back of the book enabling a student to work without a teacher.

E-Books

The Bruce Arnold series of instructional E-books is for the student who wishes to target specific areas of study that are of particular interest. Many of these books are excerpted from other larger texts. The excerpted source is listed for each book. These books are available on-line at www.muse-eek.com as well as at many e-tailers throughout the internet. These books can also be purchased in the traditional book binding format. (See the ISBN number for proper format)

Chord Velocity: Volume One, Learning to switch between chords quickly

E-book ISBN 1-890944-88-2 Traditional Book Binding ISBN 1-890944-97-1

The first hurdle a beginning guitarist encounters is difficulty in switching between chords quickly enough to make a chord progression sound like music. This book provides exercises that help a student gradually increase the speed with which they change chords. Special free audio files are also available on the muse-eek.com website to make practice more productive and fun. With a few weeks, remarkable improvement by can be achieved using this method. This book is excerpted from "1st Steps for a Beginning Guitarist Volume One."

Guitar Technique: Volume One, Learning the basics to fast, clean, accurate and fluid performance skills.

E-book ISBN 1-890944-91-2 Traditional Book Binding ISBN 1-890944-99-8

This book is for both the beginning guitarist or the more experienced guitarist who wishes to improve their technique. All aspects of the physical act of playing the guitar are covered, from how to hold a guitar to the specific way each hand is involved in the playing process. Pictures and videos are provided to help clarify each technique. These pictures and videos are either contained in the book or can be downloaded at www.muse-eek.com This book is excerpted from "1st Steps for a Beginning Guitarist Volume One."

Accompaniment: Volume One, Learning to Play Bass and Chords Simultaneously

E-book ISBN 1-890944-87-4 Traditional Book Binding ISBN 1-890944-96-3

The techniques found within this book are an excellent resource for creating and understanding how to play bass and chords simultaneously in a jazz or blues style. Special attention is paid to understanding how this technique is created, thereby enabling the student to recreate this style with other pieces of music. This book is excerpted from the book "Guitar Clinic."

Beginning Rhythm Studies: Volume One, Learning the basics of reading rhythm and playing in time.

E-book ISBN 1-890944-89-0 Traditional Book Binding 1-890944-98-X

This book covers the basics for anyone wishing to understand or improve their rhythmic abilities. Simple language is used to show the student how to read and play rhythm. Exercises are presented which can accelerate the learning process. Audio examples in the form of midifiles are available on the muse-eek.com website to facilitate learning the correct rhythm in time. This book is excerpted from the book "Rhythm Primer."

www.ingramcontent.com/pod-product-compliance
Ingram Content Group UK Ltd.
Pitfield, Milton Keynes, MK11 3LW, UK
UKHW061831190726
13855UKWH00005B/1743

9 781890 944766